INSPIRING
FINGERTIP DEVOTIONS

By AMY BOLDING

BAKER BOOK HOUSE
Grand Rapids, Michigan

ISBN: 0-8010-0558-2
Library of Congress Catalog Card Number: 75-175832

PRINTED IN THE UNITED STATES OF AMERICA

To my Father and Mother,
Rev. John Ward and Monnie Ward,
Two of God's great Christian workers

CONTENTS

1

Suitcases

"And he that earneth wages earneth wages to put it into a bag with holes." — Haggai 1:6b

Now with Christmas just over I suspect many people feel they have worked for wages and put them in a bag with holes in it.

When my husband was pastor of a small town church, it fell to my lot to take the girls from 9 to 12 years old, to camp each year. Our church owned a nice cabin on a campground belonging to our denomination.

Each summer we would arrive at the cabin, hot, tired, and loaded with all sizes and shapes of suitcases. These suitcases were borrowed, usually from bigger brothers or sisters or from parents.

I always stood back in amazement as twenty girls unpacked. You would not believe what a girl could put into a suitcase, when she was going to be gone from home three days.

Always a few felt a camp was a place where people starved. They filled at least half their suitcases with cookies, candies, crackers and pickles. Needless to say such girls were popular with the other girls at bedtime.

Some of the bags were filled with neatly folded clothes put there by a loving mother who wanted her little girl to look neat and attractive while she was away from home.

After the first flurry of hanging up dresses and borrowing coat hangers, most of the bags looked as if a small tornado had struck unexpectedly.

Often I would groan to myself and under my breath say, "If only her mother could see her now!"

How different we act at times when we are far from the restraining influences of our loved ones and the suitcase of life is there before us to be opened. Would we always be proud of the way we hung our daily lives on the coat hangers of activities?

Does a small tornado of feeling free from home ties beset us when we are about to unpack in a new place?

A New Year with all the hopes and fears of the unknown future is out before us. We cannot choose all that will face us this year, we can choose how we will react to our problems and cares.

One of the children I took to camp, always forgot to pack her Bible. Each girl was required to have one in the study sessions.

"I didn't have room in my bag for a Bible," she would excuse herself. "I will look on with Janie."

It was really her choice to leave her Bible at home. She had so many other things to fill her limited space.

At the close of an old year we cannot look on with Janie! We are responsible for all the things we deliberately left out.

In the early fifties many large stiff petticoats were in style for a time. These would not go into the suitcases. The girls would roll them up, pull a nylon hose over them and carry them on the outside of the suitcases.

Oh, we were a beautiful, gay, funny sight as we arrived at camp. Some would not unpack until they had run to the nearby cabins to see if girls from other towns had arrived.

Some wise man made this statement: Our days are like identical suitcases — all the same size — but some people can pack more into them than others.

So we are all given a New Year with suitcases or days all identical. How will we fill them?

Like the girls who enjoyed bedtime snacks, will we fill our days thinking only of the goodies of life? There are so many pleasures and good times to take our money and time. As long as we are indulging in them we will be popular with some people.

Thinking of one child who always packed a few joke books and a magic trick or two, I wonder if we will spend our days just seeing the funny side of things.

How well I remember a girl just on the verge of young womanhood, who had packed a bottle of her big sister's perfume. When the suitcase was opened she found that the perfume had spilled and made circles on her dresses.

The suitcase of life is like that. We put in some evil deeds, some jealousy, some greed, some envy — and it spills over and soils everything inside.

When I was younger I was a busy worker in the W.M.S. Once at a board meeting in Dallas, all the women were trying to check out at one time. The desk clerk was about going crazy trying to please all of the ladies and yet get his money collected.

One of the women rushed in and began pushing ahead of the others, saying as she did so, "I'm catching a ride home with some women from another hotel and I must be through and out front when they come."

We stood aside, not too gracefully, and let her finish so she could rush outside and catch her ride. The car she was to ride in pulled up to the curb just as she went through the swinging door. In her hurry she was carrying her own bag. Just as she stepped out, the door caught her suitcase and it was flung out onto the walk. It burst open. I will not tell you how everything looked, spread all over the walk. Well, there it was for all to see.

Life is like that; at times when we impose on others, it backfires and others see us as we really are.

Before you can pack any kind of a suitcase, you must open it. To put the most and best into the days of the coming year you must be open-minded and alert.

Most of us like to have a few new things to take on a trip. We can try to fill our days with many good new thoughts.

You do not stand still, either you are growing or deteriorating. Pack in some new knowledge each day. Read the Bible, some good books. Cultivate new friends.

Many of us are like the little girls with the big petticoats. We have burdened our life with extra things which are not worth the space they take. We cannot take everything along in life; so we should choose and pack carefully. We should not let some habits, like looking at too much T.V. or going on pleasure outings, take too much of our time.

The year before you is to be a year of your life. You will have only one chance to fill it with good, better, or best activities. Your children will not be the same next year as they are this; learn to enjoy each precious moment of their lives.

At the end of three days in camp I was always exhausted. With amusement I would watch and help the girls try to get everything back into their suitcases for the trip home. The popular lament was, Oh I wish I had not brought so much!

Will you at the end of the year be saying, "Oh, I wish I had not spent time on this or that; I wish I could live the time over."

You each have twenty-four hours in your days. See how well you can pack them.

2

So—Make Your Move!

My father often made us laugh when we were children by telling the following story.

He and my mother were newlyweds. They often went to visit some of the relatives in the evenings and returned home late. One night they stepped into the dark house and before my father could strike a match (that being the era of oil lamps), in the moonlight he saw a man standing in front of him.

"What are you doing here?" he called out. The man replied not a word.

"Answer me or I'll knock you down," my father said in a very loud voice.

Still no answer, so he reached for a chair to hit the man. As he picked up the chair he noticed the man picked up a chair also. He put his chair down and the man put his chair down.

"Sweetheart, I almost broke your new mirror," he told my mother as he at last found a match and lighted the lamp.

"We know the secret." We would laugh, "You were afraid of yourself."

How often in life we are afraid of ourselves. We fail in some things because we are afraid of a reflected image.

A movement my father made warned him he was being

foolish. In life we do not always have a warning when we are about to make a foolish move.

In the story of the Prodigal Son we read, "I will arise and go to my father, and will say unto Him, Father, I have sinned against 'heaven, and before thee" (Luke 15:18). This was not an easy move for the young man to make. He had left home rich and proud, he returned humble and ashamed. Yet his return brought happiness to his father, peace to his own heart, and a wonderful lesson for all of God's wandering children for ages to come.

So — make your move!

Every person needs to make some type of move. Maybe you are not a prodigal living in sin and shame. You might be just an ordinary person who tries to live right each day. Is there a move you need to make? Can you honestly say you need to move in any direction for the better?

In a college class the professor passed out a sheet of paper with questions about the personal life of the pupils. One young lady rated herself 99 percent perfect. When he had looked over the papers the teacher wrote on the pupil's paper: "Study yourself more closely, only one perfect person has ever lived on this earth."

As I write I think of so many moves I need to make: moves for a better prayer life, moves for more unselfish giving, moves for helping others, moves for witnessing for Christ.

Looking closely I see times when I have been looking in the mirror at a false enemy. My road to a better and more useful life seems very, very long. The only way to begin is to forge ahead. Make your move, you will receive power from on high if it is the right move.

Move up — to higher ideals.

Move on — to greater work for the Master.

Move out — to find new fields of service.

Move ahead — to the greatest time in your life.

Now

3

Can You Answer the Question?

Miss English looked into the faces of her First Grade pupils. All seemed alert and eager to learn, except one. She asked a simple question and all hands waved eagerly, except one.

"Jane, can you answer the question?" she asked the one whose hand had not been raised. "Jane?"

The second time her name was called Jane looked up.

"Miss English I saw a mother bird and a baby bird in a cage on Mrs. Brown's front porch." Jane seemed oblivious to the snickers of the other children. "Do you suppose the father bird is away fighting a war like my daddy?"

Miss English, being a good teacher, recognized the fact that Jane was troubled by greater problems and questions than the ones she had to ask. She made plans to help the child in private.

In this day of troubled times we often ponder questions we cannot answer. We have only one place to go for the answer to our problems.

In Judges 18:5 we find that the tribe of Dan had sent out men to seek an inheritance for their tribe. Coming to a man who was hired as a priest they said to him:

". . . Ask counsel, we pray thee, of God, that we may know whether our way which we shall go shall be prosperous."

How often in life we make decisions, plan moves and execute them without ever asking God for an answer to the question, "Is this the right thing to do, the right way to go?"

We cannot answer all of life's questions. We do not need to answer them without help and counsel.

A young man away in college made an expenditure of over one hundred dollars, without asking his parents' permission. What he did not realize was the fact that the parents were almost going hungry to keep him in school. They could not honor such a large check for something he did not especially need.

When his father refused to honor the check, the young man was very angry and felt his parents were unkind.

He failed to ask before he made his decision to spend money. He had to get a job on the side and work out the debt.

How many unhappy situations would be avoided if we would only answer a few questions before we make decisions.

"Ask of me, and I shall give thee the heathen for thine inheritance, and the uttermost parts of the earth for thy possessions" (Ps. 2:8).

God's promises still hold true for His children today. We fail because we think we can answer all questions and we neglect to ask the Father.

A small child in school sat and pondered on a problem. The teacher passing by his desk saw his blank paper and asked: "Billy, don't you understand the question?"

"No, Miss Brown, I do not understand what this word means."

"Why that word is comprehend, it means to understand." The teacher then explained to the whole class the meaning of the problem they had been asked to solve. She was glad to explain. They had just been slow to let her know their difficulty.

So it is in the life of a Christian, we try to answer the questions in our life alone. All the time our Heavenly Father wants us to confide in Him and ask Him for an answer.

William Cullen Bryant wrote:

14

Can You Answer the Question?

> He, who, from zone to zone,
> Guides through the boundless sky thy certain flight,
> In the long way that I must tread alone
> Will lead my steps aright.

In all lives there will come troubles, sorrow, and reverses. At such times we have many questions we long to have answered. In our human frailties we cannot answer the questions that come to us in such times. At times we wait many months or years before we feel we have even a part answer to our problems.

Even the great preacher and writer, Paul, faced questions he could not answer. In I Corinthians 13:12 he write, "For now we see through a glass, darkly; but then face to face: now I know in part; but then shall I know even as I also am known."

Can you answer the question? Why are some rich and others poor, why are some well while others are ill, why are some happy and others sad?

We will never in this life be able to answer the many questions which bother us. Then how can we go on, not knowing why things happen?

We can go on happy and glad if we are children of God, for we do know one answer, He doeth all things well. Knowing this and resting secure in His love, we do not need to know the answer to all questions.

> "In 'Pastures Green' not always — sometimes, He
> Who knoweth best, in sorrow leadeth me
> Thro' weary ways, where heavy shadows be, —
>
> "Out of the sunshine warm and soft and bright,
> Out of the sunshine into darkest night.
> I oft would faint with sorrow and affright,
>
> "Only for this; I know He holds my hand
> And tho' the way be thro' a dark and dreary land
> I trust, altho I may not understand.
>
> "So, down the shadowy vale my lonely way I go
> And in the hereafter I shall know
> Why in His wisdom He hath led me so."
> — Author Unknown

15

Can you answer the question?

You may not answer the questions of life and its problems but with a few simple rules you can live with the questions.

The first rule is, a firm and unshakable belief in Christ as our Lord.

The second rule is, talk with God each day and place your problems in His hands.

The third rule, read the Bible every day and see what God has to tell you through its pages.

The fourth rule. Forget yourself, live to serve others.

The fifth rule, if you have gone by the above four suggestions, then rest secure in the right outcome and be happy and content.

4

Your Life!
A Minimum or a Maximum!

A man came to visit in our home. We had known his family many years before so we asked about the different brothers. As we talked of different ones he came to his brother Aaron.

"I am sorry to say Aaron lives a minimum life."

"What do you mean, a minimum life?" we asked, curious.

"He majors on so many small things, he never thinks of the really maximum things in life."

Often in the years that followed our friend's visit we would catch ourselves being too concerned with small problems or cares. We would stop with a sigh and say: "We must live a maximum life, forget the minimum things."

"He that observeth the wind shall not sow; and he that regardeth the clouds shall not reap" (Eccles. 11:4).

Once, for a period of two years, I went around more dead than alive, because I refused to go to the hospital and have an operation I needed to make me well. I was afraid, I might go to sleep and not wake up. I might need blood and would have to ask friends to give theirs. I might be ill a long time and be unable to pay the bill. So many, many things I kept thinking of, and I refused to go. Why didn't I think more of the one big thing: I would be well and normal again?

At last the day came when I had to face the big question.

Did I want to live or die? I wanted to live so I passed over the small problems and went to the hospital. In two weeks I was home. I had not needed blood. I had money enough to pay the bill. I had been asleep for a few hours but I awoke to a new life, a healthy useful happy life.

So many people go on in a life of sin because they major on all the minimum problems. So many say, "I am afraid I cannot be faithful all the time."

Peter was not faithful all the time, yet Christ loved him and forgave his faults and sins.

If we magnify all the difficulties in life we will live in a very minimum way. It is the farmer who goes on sowing and reaping in spite of threatening weather, who makes the good crops.

I once knew a young lady who was well educated, nice enough looking, and had some friends. She refused to take a job because each one she heard about had some little hardship or problem. She would always say, "I'll wait for just the right opportunity."

As a young woman she could have gotten work and grown into better positions. While she refused to work and lived off her parents, she grew old. When her parents died, she was forced to take any position she could get in order to survive.

"Now when they saw the boldness of Peter and John, and perceived that they were unlearned and ignorant men, they marvelled; and took knowledge of them, that they had been with Jesus" (Acts 4:13).

Peter and John could have said to each other, "We do not know as much about world affairs as some people, we have never travelled far or been around the world with a tour group; perhaps we should just go about and in a minimum way tell a few people about Christ."

They wanted to live a maximum life, they wanted to be bold. Why? Because they had been with Jesus. He set an example of boldness, of doing the most for the most people.

18

If he met a funeral he brought the corpse back to life, If he met a blind man He opened his eyes, To see a need was to fill that need.

As Christians we so often say, "I'll do a task if no one else will."

We too often want to be called Christians, but we want to live just the least possible life of service.

While we were traveling in Northeastern Oklahoma we kept seeing signs about glass factories. We decided to stop at one to see how glass was blown into vases. We were amazed at one table filled with vases for only a small amount of money. We purchased a large box full. What wonderful gifts these would make for Christmas.

When Christmas time came I started unpacking my box of vases. All but a few were broken. I was very disappointed. I wished we had paid more and bought the ones which had been fired longer. We could not go back to the glass factory because it was several hundred miles away.

How often in life we choose the minimum in place of the maximum, only to look back later and wish we had paid a higher price. Life also, when once passed cannot be called back.

Usefulness, happiness, love, service, choose the maximum way each day.

> Minimum? or maximum? which will it be?
> Which will you choose for your life?
> Happiness? sorrow? bond slave or free?
> Peace and contentment or strife?
>
> Be such a blessing to others each day
> That you would be truly missed
> Not just some good but the best in your way,
> Needs to be on your "do list."
>
> It isn't enough to be busy
> And driving yourself all the time
> It isn't enough to do good things
> Which aren't really worth a thin dime.

19

Why not be your best every moment
Your maximum self every day
And turn from that minimum living
With zest for the finest alway.
— J. T. Bolding

5

Something Free

We were very excited over a trip. We had been invited to spend three days at a very plush resort for retired people. We were not retired but we were only two years from retirement. We were invited with all expenses paid except our food.

It seemed the time would never come. We imagined ourselves fishing, playing games, and just taking life easy, far away from a telephone, for three whole days.

When we went to register at the office we were told there was one requirement. We must take time to drive over the grounds with a salesman next day. We agreed.

Right then and there we should have declined the invitation, gotten in our car, and gone to a motel on a river bank some place.

We wandered around, on our own, that first afternoon, looking at the wonderful trees and lakes. The evening we spent resting and looking at Television.

Next morning we went to keep our appointment with the guide who was to show us the grounds. The guide turned out to be a super salesman, with a number of years practice at high pressure sales.

By sheer will power and determination we managed to get out of his clutches after two-and-one-half hours.

Rain started pouring down and it was too late in the day

or we would have packed up and left. We packed our bags and set an alarm. At five next morning we left. We could have stayed one more night but the whole visit was a bitter experience because of pressure by the salesman.

Were those two nights we stayed free? No! We were forced to spend two-and-one-half hours of our very limited vacation time in a way we did not like. We were terribly embarrassed and all the fun was taken away.

"There is nothing free in this world," my husband said as we drove along over wet roads. "If you ever receive another invitation in the mail about something free, burn it."

"It reminds me of a time when I was a child and a store advertised free candy and balloons for children," I said. "My mother dressed me up pretty and I wore a small cross on a chain. I had received the cross for attending Sunday School a certain number of Sundays. It was my dearest possession. After we returned home my cross was missing. So I paid a very dear price for a few cents worth of candy."

The whole world is running after offers of something for free. Nations want free trade with other nations. People want free favors with friends and neighbors. Many people want to live free off the taxes others pay.

"And thou shalt take no gift: for the gift blindeth the wise, and perverteth the words of the righteous" (Exod. 23:8).

A Judge in a court of law received an expensive gift from a man who was coming to trial on a serious charge. The judge sent the gift back to him because he did not want to be obligated in any way.

It is common knowledge in our land today that many law makers are influenced by people who lobby for certain causes.

We should be very careful about gifts we give and gifts we receive. Will we pay for them in the future by letting our decisions be influenced?

"A wicked man taketh a gift out of the bosom to pervert the ways of judgment" (Prov. 17:23).

"A man's gift maketh room for him, and bringeth him before great men" (Prov. 18:16).

There are different kinds of gifts. There are the gifts we call bribes, gifts with strings attached. Gifts from which we hope to reap rewards or favors. The motives for such gifts are not usually the best.

Then there are the gifts of love and kindness. We like to give gifts to those we love. We often give gifts to our church or to charitable institutions because we want to show our gratitude to God for His blessings.

I have heard ministers talk about receiving expensive gifts from members of their congregations. Other ministers from poorer churches at times envy their more fortunate friends. Yet I knew a minister who took many gifts from a wealthy member. Then a time of some grave decisions came. The minister did not see eye to eye with his benefactor. Yet such pressure was placed on him that he gave his sanction to something he knew to be wrong. His teen-age son was so repulsed by his father's action he became bitter and as soon as he was old enough he left home.

There is one gift that is free to all men, one gift that will always bring joy and happiness, the gift of God's Son. Christ died that we might have salvation.

Yet if we are to be happy with the gift of Salvation we will seek to show our love by serving.

A friend brought me some very nice tomatoes. They were out of season and quite a treat. Do you know what I did? I wrapped part of a fresh baked cake and urged her to accept it.

She did not bring the tomatoes in order to get the cake; she didn't know I had just baked it. She brought her gift out of a heart of love. I gave her some cake to show her my gratitude and appreciation.

Christ did not die in order to get what we had to give. He died to pay our debt of sin, yet if we love Him we want to live a life of service in return.

Little Is Really for Free

There are hundreds of gimmicks in practice
    In business about us today,
And so many pretend to be giving
    Something of great value away.

Now the reason for this situation
    Is simple and easy to see:
Nearly all of us seem to be hoping
    That we will get something for free.

The poor fish who is tempted for dinner
    To grab handy baits easy fare,
Should be warned of the hook that is hidden,
    And cautioned that he should beware.

Now in spite of the generous offers,
    Advice, good for you and for me:
There's a hook in the world's propositions,
    And really, there's little for free.

— J. T. Bolding

6

Help Wanted

"For God hath power to help, and to cast down."
— II Chronicles 25:8c

Hide not thy face far from me; put not thy servant away in anger: thou hast been my help; leave me not, neither forsake me, O God of my salvation. — Psalm 26:9

Three widows live in the same block in a small town. They are old and have no children living near. They often look at television together. As they visit the cry of each is, "I need help." One is constantly running short of money. She has the same sized pension as the others so they do not offer to help her.

One of the widows has a large yard and she is always in need of help in keeping her yard.

One is desperately afraid at night, yet she does not have the money to pay someone to stay with her at night.

All three could go to a nursing home and be well cared for, but that is not their choice of a way to live.

A friend of mine lost his job. He frantically searched the Help Wanted pages of the newspaper. He asked many of our friends to help him locate work.

Our whole world today is crying for *help* of one kind or another.

Many cry for help in their love life. The people who term themselves counselors are very busy all the time.

Ministers find the world crying for spiritual help. They must spend much of their time and effort trying to show a lost world that God is ready to help.

Our town is far enough south, so we seldom have ice on the lakes. Early in 1971 we had a very cold spell. A small lake in the park froze over. The children had a great time. This was a new experience for them, skating on ice.

The weather grew warmer and the ice began to melt. The older boys began to play football again in the park. A woman walking alone by the lake saw a small boy skate out on the ice. She called to him to come back but he didn't heed her call. Suddenly he fell through the ice. The woman began to scream for help. She ran to the big boys playing ball.

One of the boys ran to call the fire department. One ran out on the ice, he saw he too would fall in, so he got down on his stomach and crawled to the edge of the hole. He managed to grab the child's clothing and pulled him out. The child was unconscious. The big boy managed to pull and push the unconscious child to a small island. There he worked giving mouth to mouth resuscitation. Soon a large crowd had gathered on the shore and were shouting encouragement.

The fire truck arrived and managed to get both boys off the island and into an ambulance. Both boys lived and were soon well, because a woman cried, "Help."

The three widow ladies need help, they want help with their problems. Because they are old and tired they put forth very little effort to change their plight. They cry and pray alone in the night. To the public they put on a brave front. Is the world filled with many people who need help spiritually, yet as far as we can see they are self-sufficient?

My friend who searched the Help Wanted ads knew he needed a position. He told his friends of his need. Then he worked at going about applying for positions in every place possible.

We can help answer the call for *help* from those about us. First of all, we can pray for our friends, neighbors, and enemies. After we have prayed for them the Holy Spirit will lead us to take some action.

If we pray for others we will just naturally love others. To love is to want to share, to share is to grow bigger and stronger as a person.

The people in the world could be described as walking Help Wanted ads. Very few people do not need help in some area of life.

There is a great secret about the call for help. Those who get busy about answering the call from others find their own lives being filled to the brim with happiness and satisfaction.

A young woman went to a city to find work. She expected the man she loved to follow in a few months.

After a few months his letters were fewer and farther apart. The girl was distressed but she was too proud to ask anyone she knew in her home community to tell her what was wrong.

One day a letter came from the young man's father. He told her the son had become ill soon after she left and had finally died. He had made all his friends and family keep the secret of his illness because he wanted her to keep her job.

With a broken heart the girl prayed for help in her grief. God led a man to ask her to attend a mission church where he worked. In the little mission she found many places she could be a help and a blessing.

We often must answer our own need for help by seeking to lose our lives serving others.

Every time you see a death wreath on a door, you may know that inside that door there are people needing help to face the loss of a loved one. We can give sympathy.

Some people read the Help Wanted ads in the paper out of curiosity. They just enjoy knowing who needs help. They have no idea of answering the ads.

So in life, many people flock to the bank to watch someone drown. They will shout encouragement but never reach out to pull them to shore. We need to examine our lives often and be sure we are not standing unheeding as the call for help goes out.

My Lord

My Lord has been so good to me:
    He blotted out my sin;
He brought salvation full and free,
    And gave me peace within.

With hope and joy he filled my life,
    So wondrous and so grand;
He soothed my heart's continual strife;
    Now we walk hand in hand.

In blessed confidence I live;
    My heart o'erflows each day;
My all I daily try to give
    To brighten someone's way.
              — J. T. Bolding

7

Skyline of Life

"And while they looked steadfastly toward heaven as he went up, behold, two men stood by them in white apparel." — Acts 1:10

We think of the sky as the apparent arch of the heaven, extending from horizon to horizon. We often speak of the skyline of a city. Most of us are familiar with the skyline of our favorite city.

We have a skyline in life. A line we keep looking forward to. To a man growing old, his skyline seems to be the day he retires from regular work. To a musician his skyline seems to be far off in the distance when he reaches fame and fortune.

The day Christ ascended into the heavens, His followers stood and gazed into the sky. They could see their leader going farther and farther out of sight. They were alone again! This time Christ left them with a vision of things to accomplish before they too would join Him in the palaces beyond.

We made a trip to the Eastern states one summer. People kept telling us: Be sure to drive down the Blue Ridge Parkway.

We were eager to see this famous drive and enjoy it. Going up on the drive late in the afternoon we were amazed at the beauty of the valley below, at the shrubs and flowers all along the road.

We saw a place we could spend the night and stopped. As dark settled about us, we sat for a long time looking at the lights in the valley below. We felt we were spending the night on the skyline of the world.

Climbers want to reach the skyline of a distant peak, writers want a byline in a paper or magazine. Every human being with an ounce of get-up-and-go wants to reach some goal.

Just like the disciples we often spend time gazing aloft at heights we think we cannot attain. Yet all the time if we want to reach the skyline of our life's ambitions, we must turn to the ones near at hand and start there to climb.

Older people often look at the youth in this strange generation and say, They have no goal in life, they cannot see the skyline above them.

Yes, they have a goal. They are the children of a generation of extremely busy parents. Parents more interested in making money than in being with their offspring. The hippies seek what they think is love and recognition.

The skyline of their lives is something they think they could not find at home. Rebellion never helped reach the top. It only frustrates and dooms.

We have traveled many times down a valley road in New Mexico. We call it the Apple Valley road because on each side of the road for a number of miles we see apple trees. Many roadside stands advertise apples for sale. We are not traveling to see the apple trees, we are looking at the mountains on each side of the valley. We know we must get around the mountains and on the west side if we are to reach California and visit our loved ones there.

There is no road across the mountains, we must go around. Often in life we seek a destination and are discouraged because there is no road going that way, we must go around.

Always before us we see the skyline of our hopes and ambitions. Most people take a lifetime to reach the height.

Why?

We will see something just a little higher beckoning the farther we go. The joy of life is in the going.

An artist friend of mine tells me we see what we want to see. She often gets up early and tries to paint the sunrise. She is old and in her mind she has a vision of the sunset and the sunrise meeting some place in the unknown. To her that will be the way with the end of her life. The setting of the sun on earth and the rising of the sun in Heaven.

After we have driven through Apple Valley and past the high mountains we see far ahead of us a water tower. We know this water tower is the highest thing in the next town. Just a water tower shining in the sun, the only thing to be seen on the skyline. We know it represents a place where we can find food and shelter for the night. It says to us, Keep driving, soon you will be in a cool room and have rest for the night.

A mother and small daughter in Detroit were given a mongrel dog. They called the dog, Salty, and lavished much love on her. Neighbors complained and so the dog was given to some people three hundred miles away who would see that she had a place to run and romp.

Salty looked toward the city of Detroit and ran away from her country home. After two weeks of hard travel she arrived back on the doorstep of her former owner. She was almost starved, her paws were bleeding, and she was very dirty, but she was back where she wanted to be.

People sometimes are not as persistent about struggling to reach their skyline of ambition as Salty was. We give up too easily.

One morning my husband called me to the east window in our kitchen.

"Look at that range of mountains!" he exclaimed.

There in the east was a perfect appearing range of mountains with the sun just beginning to make light behind them.

Now we live in a flat country where there are no hills, let alone mountains, so I knew his mountains were clouds.

Often we look and see clouds on our skyline which look so real, we set our goal to reach them, but like my husband's mountains they vanish in a few hours to be seen no more.

It Can Be Done

Say not, my son: "It can't be done!" —
    First try! with a grit of your teeth!
It can be done, but only by one
    Who will never admit defeat.

No failure can be — as you will see —
    If you try, with your head held high.
There's no such thing that life can bring,
    Except through your ceasing to try.

If the cause is right you'll win your fight.
    No matter what the odds may be —
So with all your might, stand for the right.
    And — like truth — it will set you free.

If the blows come fast and seem to last
    'Til endurance has reached its end —
Forget the past! and hold on fast,
    With a tilt to your manly chin.

Say not, my son: "It can't be done!" —
    First try! with a grit of your teeth!
It can be done, but only by one
    Who will never admit defeat.
            — Edward V. Wood

8

Inspection Station

"Ye shall know them by their fruits. Do men gather grapes of thorns, or figs of thistles?" — Matthew 7:16
"Wherefore by their fruits ye shall know them."
— Matthew 7:20

My husband and I were driving along looking at the bare expanses of country on all sides. If the good, hard surface road had not been in front of us we would have thought ourselves lost in a wilderness. There were no houses, no stores, no people, except the ones rushing by in cars.

You may have guessed where we were. Going across part of New Mexico toward Arizona. Then we saw a sign, All cars must stop one-half mile ahead.

As we came nearer we saw a sign which read, Inspection Station.

It felt so good to drive under the shelter at the station and be out of the burning rays of the sun. I jumped out to walk a moment and rest my legs. My husband was asked to open the trunk of the car.

"Have you any fruit in this car?"

"No."

"Have you anything growing, like a plant?"

"No."

"Fine, you may drive on."

Soon we were back out on the road again and other cars were stopping at the inspection station.

We were hastening on to what we hoped would be a happy holiday.

The thought of the great Inspection Station we were to face in the future came to my mind.

But why dost thou judge thy brother? or why dost thou set at nought thy brother? for we shall all stand before the judgment seat of Christ (Rom. 14:10).

All travelers come to inspection stations occasionally. Some are stations looking for fruit. Some, at borders of nations, are inspecting for drug and smuggled goods. Inspection stations are to be expected and planned for.

People have all kinds of ways they try to get by the inspectors. Some have been caught trying to smuggle drugs from one country to another by putting them in the spare tire of their automobile. One family coming near the fruit inspection station, stopped, ate all the oranges they could, then peeled the ones left and put them in their portable ice chest.

They were so gorged on oranges before the day was over it was several months before they would eat another one.

When we stand before the great judgment seat of our Lord, we will be asked, Do you have any fruit?

If we do not have any fruit we will be sad because we will not hear the words, Well done, thou good and faithful servant.

There is a certain fruit farm in California where many of the regular travelers plan to stop. The fruit store is high on a hill overlooking the busy freeway. The ones who wish to buy fruit must turn off the busy road and take a narrow road leading to the store.

So a Christian, if he would find fruit, must turn aside from the rush and busyness of life and seek the lost, the tired, the weary, the discouraged.

In seeking the lost, in telling the story of Jesus, we find our own lives renewed and revived.

After traveling a few hundred miles west from the Arizona inspection station, we came to the border of California and another station.

This time we were prepared for the inspection. We took our time, emptied the litter from the car into a large trash barrel, pulled over out of the way and drank some of the good cold water we found inside the station.

Often in life we will feel refreshed and cleansed if we take time to inspect our daily activities. Put the litter and filth in the trash. Take a fresh vow unto the Lord and go on our way to find fruit for the Master's use.

We sometimes get so busy we forget we are fruit pickers and not pleasure seekers.

A very popular man about town spent his Sundays on the golf course, his Saturday nights getting drunk, and his week days making sharp business deals.

One day trouble in the form of a daughter's divorce caused him to stop at an "inspection station" and look at his own life. He was not pleased with what he saw. He saw his family breaking up and in sorrow and he had no strength to give them.

In desperation he sought a conference with a minister. After much patient counseling on the part of the minister the man was won to faith in Christ.

The very next week on his day off he appeared at the church and asked, "What do Christians do on their day off?"

The pastor picked three cards from his prospect file. "Go and visit these people and tell them what God has done for you."

Soon the people in that church began to notice a change in the service. People were being saved. One man was taking his day off to tell others about Christ. The man had inspected his life, found it lacking, and made a change for a better life. Then he started bearing fruit.

If I But Knew You Better

If I but knew you better
    I'm sure that I would find
The heart that is within you
    Is just as good as mine.

Your thoughts I cannot measure
    By drawing down a line,
To circumscribe your thinking,
    And make it just like mine —

I cannot break in upon
    The secrets of your soul —
And weigh the treasures of your house
    To say they're not gold.

The thoughts that course within you —
    And what you think and plan,
I have no right to judge them,
    Nor has any other man.

'Tis God alone can judge you,
    And say if you are good.
I could not measure your mind
    Not even if I would.

But if I knew you better
    I'm sure that I would find
The heart that is within you
    Is just as good as mine.
                — Edward V. Wood

9

Your Contribution

"Can a man be profitable unto God, as he that is wise may be profitable unto himself?" — Job 22:2

If we could always remember we have a contribution to make to the world, we would be more useful.

A man and his wife became ill. They went from doctor to doctor and their friends wondered which one would die first. The doctors could find nothing really wrong with either of them.

Then their daughter-in-law was killed in an accident. The broken-hearted son brought his two small children to his parents, "Just until I can make some arrangements."

The couple became so engrossed with taking care of the little grandchildren they forgot to be sick.

What happened? They became busy making a contribution to others.

People must have faith in their ability to make a contribution to the world, to those in need about them.

It sometimes take courage to stand up and live for a purpose. It takes faith in one's ability to live for that purpose.

An inventor must have faith in his invention if he is to succeed. A writer must have faith in his ability to write what people need to read.

People who have no faith in themselves seldom make worthwhile contributions to the world.

Each thumbprint, they tell us, is different. People can be identified by their fingerprints because the authorities have confidence that they are different.

So each person is different, has a different contribution to make to the world.

A contribution to the good of those about us brings satisfaction with life. Just as the couple became ill when they felt they were no longer needed in the world, so most people become unhappy if they do not contribute to life.

Where would mankind be without faith in the contributions of the world about us.

What good would the contribution of money be if we had no faith in the good of the currency? What contribution could religion make in the world if no one believed.

You must believe you have a contribution to offer, then seek to make that contribution.

An old friend called one day. He was in great distress about a college-age son. The son was planning to quit school at the end of the term and go away with the Peace Corps. Our friend owned rich farmlands and cattle. He wanted his son to follow in his footsteps.

We invited the boy to come out for a visit and some home-cooked food. Then we spent the afternoon talking about very serious things. One thing the college student said stayed with us.

"I want to make some kind of a contribution to the world with my life," he said. "And this seems to be the way I am impressed to go."

We admired the boy because in the face of much opposition from friends and family, he stood firm in what he believed. In time he did go to Africa to spend some years as a Peace Corps worker. He had the courage to live for a purpose! In spite of hardship and opposition, he did what gave him peace of mind and a sense of satisfaction with himself.

Man's Blessings Three

Three things a man must have to live
    A life that's full and free,
And lacking one he cannot give
    His best — nor greatness see:

Good health is named as number one,
    And well it is there placed.
For he who's ill from sun to sun
    But runs a limping race.

Then there's a need of one to love —
    Who does a love return —
For this the Loving God above
    Has made our souls to yearn.

Then taking health and love in hand —
    Cementing them through toil,
Occupation blesses man
    As sunshine blesses soil.
                — Edward V. Wood

10

That Dog Next Door

"Devise not evil against thy neighbor, seeing he dwelleth by thee." — Proverbs 3:29

"Envy thou not the oppressor, and choose none of his ways." — Proverbs 3:31

For ten years we lived in a modest home on the south side of our town. We watched the neighbor children grow up and finish school. We liked our house and the location.

Then one day the house next door sold. The new people were very loud and used lots of profanity. The houses were so close we could not help hearing. Often at night the children in the new family came home very late and we would be awakened by their loud talk.

The straw that broke the camel's back, as far as we were concerned, was when the man next door bought a dog. We do not dislike dogs, but there are all kinds of dogs. This dog was one with a loud bark. Sometimes he barked almost all night.

It so happened that the dog owner built a pen very near our bedroom window. We were awake more than we were asleep.

What will we do? was our most frequent question.

We decided to move away from our troubles. We put our

home on the market and while we waited for it to sell we planned a new home.

We bought a lot in an addition far out from town. There was a small house next door to our lot but it lacked ten or twelve feet coming to our line.

With vacant lots all around us, we began to enjoy the peace and quiet of living in our new home. We had left the dog next door far across town.

Then one of our West Texas sand storms came. The sand was so thick in the atmosphere we could barely see across the street. There were no houses close by to help keep the sand down, there were no grassy yards and trees to break the sweep of red sand.

We had problems in our new paradise!

Man has had problems with his paradise since time began and Eve met the tempter.

We cannot keep moving and moving and ever find peace. We must face some problems and live with them.

A young college professor was always seeing "dogs" next door in his job. He would arrive at a school, thrilled with his job. After a few months he would get the idea he was not getting the proper respect from his superiors. He would complain to his wife. She would tell everyone she met that her husband was being mistreated. In just a year or two they would be moving to get away from the "dog" next door. They failed to realize they were taking the dog with them because they had the same attitude in the next place.

For none of us liveth to himself, and no man dieth to himself (Rom. 14:7).

We often hear the statement, "It's a small world." As far as people are concerned the world is getting smaller all the time.

In 1900 a trip to New York from Texas was an event of very few people's lifetime. The ones who were able to go to the biggest city in our country, were looked up to as paragons of knowledge. Today people can fly to New York, spend several hours and be back in time for dinner.

Once we only heard about the problems of the world, now they are the "dog" next door to us.

After living in my new home for a year, a new family moved into the house nearest to us. A widow with a small boy. She really had problems. On trying to encourage and help her, I found that blessings can be had from trying to help those next to us.

We are a part of society and no matter how far we move or how much we shut our doors to those around us we still have an obligation to others.

The "dog" next door that makes our life miserable, may take many shapes and forms. No man lives unto himself and no man dies unto himself.

In our world today we find many problems with liquor and drugs. At times we think degradation and crime are so prevalent we cannot possibly cope with the problems.

According to a study made by Senator Robert C. Byrd, in Washington, D.C., 40 percent of relief checks are cashed in liquor stores.

What can we do about such a monstrous "dog" next door as that?

We can vote against liquor every chance we get. We can seek out the alcoholic and try to help him stop drinking.

As long as we live there will be "dogs" next door in some form. As Christians we can pray and work to make the world and our community better places to live.

Night Stroll

I wandered forth beneath the stars
One balmy summer night;
As insects strummed on their guitars
I thought of God and right.

I walked alone o'er hill and vale: —
My mind confused and tired;

It seemed my hopes had all gone stale
And naught my soul inspired.

I raised my eyes unto the skies,
And felt my problems fade,
For difficulty often dies
When at God's feet it's laid.

I came again, refreshed and glad;
My fears had crept away;
The right solution now I had
With which to greet the day.
— J. T. Bolding, Sr.

11

The Avenue of Every Day Life

"As the apple tree among the trees of the wood, so is my beloved among the sons. I sat down under his shadow with great delight, and his fruit was sweet to my taste." — Song of Solomon 2:3

On the night of May 11, 1970 the town of Lubbock, Texas was a beautiful place to behold.

It was a quiet West Texas town of 170,000 people; a town where people took great pride in having beautiful homes and yards.

In the cool of the evening my husband and I sat on our front porch and watched the heavy clouds, hoping for a much-needed rain. West Texas is always hoping for rain and gets very little.

My husband, a minister, is so often away from home, I often feel lonely in the evenings. As we sat quietly looking at the flowers and trees I thought, *What a beautiful city Lubbock is.* How near to heaven it seemed to be sitting quietly together in such a beautiful place.

The dark came early because of the heavy clouds and a bit of hail started to fall. We left the porch and went inside to answer the phone.

Our daughter from California was calling to talk a bit.

44

"Your line must be bad," she said. "I can't understand you too well."

"We are having a small hail storm," we told her.

Before ten o'clock that evening the proud and beautiful city of Lubbock was brought low by a tornado, or as the experts in such matters thought, by two tornadoes.

The avenue of everyday life was changed for almost every person in the city. Twenty-six people were killed in the storm. Many more were seriously injured. A great number of people lost their homes and business establishments. The tallest building in town was twisted and cracked. Our paradise was shattered!

Churches, homes, public places were opened to the homeless. People began taking food, clothing, bedding, to these places as fast as they could.

I cannot begin to tell you about all the tall shadows people cast that evening and in the tormenting days to follow.

One story I felt was worth telling was about a boy, going to college and working nights. He had started back to the dormitory when the storm struck downtown. He took the best shelter he could find until the storm passed. He was so shocked he did not know what to do. He just breathed a prayer of thanksgiving for his life, then looked to see what he could do to be of service.

The plate glass window of a jewelry store was gone and the door blown open. The college lad went inside. Found some kind of a weapon and kept vandals away until the owner arrived next morning. The owner was unaware of the storm until he heard the early morning news.

The young man could at any time during the night, have filled his pockets with diamonds and walked away. He was a fine Christian boy and his one desire was to help someone.

A man I knew was driving down the street when the storm hit. He had presence of mind enough to turn off his ignition key. Then he crouched on the floor of the car. Every glass in his car was broken out. When the storm was over rain poured down. My friend was bleeding and wet. He went to the door of a house and asked if they could help him.

The people would not turn him away, but he could tell they were afraid of him. He prayed silently for God to show him a way to let them know he only needed help.

It came to him to mention the church to which he belonged and suggest that they all bow in a prayer of thanksgiving that they were alive.

"Can you be thankful, your car is probably a total loss?" one of those present said.

"Certainly, I am thankful, cars can be bought but human life is given only by God." Telling of the experience later the man hoped he had set the right Christian example to the people huddled there in fright.

The love of God in the hearts of people helped patch up the paradise that was once Lubbock. People too old to go and help serve food, opened their purse strings and helped provide money.

Have you ever asked yourself how you would react to some great emergency? We will not always walk a smooth and lovely avenue of life, there will come times of trial. Yet it is in these times of trial a Christian casts the tallest shadow.

The best way to be prepared to cast a tall shadow for right and righteousness in time of trial, is to cast a shadow for good each day of life.

Once I was amazed when a man I felt was a great Christian, just went to pieces at the loss of a child in an accident. All his friends were shocked. They thought he would trust in God more than ever. He stopped attending services and for many years was very bitter.

Another friend, not given to regular church attendance, lost a High School aged son in an accident. He surprised all who knew him by starting to attend services regularly. No one heard him say a word against God because of his great grief.

46

After a few months had passed someone asked him why he changed.

"I believe in God, but I have not served Him," he said. "If He had to take my boy to make me realize the kind of life I was living, I didn't want my boy to die in vain. Now I am at peace with God. He is taking care of my son in a better place."

To walk the avenue of life is to meet some times of troubles and trials. We would not want to miss living just because there might be some problems along the way.

To walk life's pathway and feel we have helped make the way better for others gives a feeling of satisfaction.

The Lord Is My Shepherd

The Lord is my living shepherd,
    And "Want" I shall never know!
Asks one: "Shall not want for what?"
    Would you really like to know?

To have no want of pleasant times —
    Nor hard times — the soul trying —
No want of times of doubt and fear,
    And of times on Him relying.

My prayer went up for strength to do —
    to achieve and to excell —
He gave instead infirmity,
    That I might thus do all things well.

I prayed for things I might enjoy —
    A good life — filled with pleasure —
Instead He gave abundant life,
    To enjoy all things without measure.

Giving nothing that I asked for —
    But — all without my knowing —
He gave everything I'd hoped for:
    A full life — overflowing!
                 — Edward V. Wood

12

Synthetic Religion

"No man can serve two masters: for either he will hate the one, and love the other; or else he will hold to the one, and despise the other. Ye cannot serve God and mammon." — Matthew 6:24

Not long ago I went to buy a frame for a picture I valued highly. I wanted a beautiful, ornate, wooden frame. The clerk showed me frames made of plastic, they looked like wood but were lighter in weight. Then he showed me frames made of a cheap type wood and covered with paper printed to look like walnut. Finally he came to the type of frame I wanted, one I felt that would last and be beautiful for many years.

Have you ever thought how much like the picture frames some people are who say they are Christians?

After teaching adult Sunday School classes many years, I have decided many people have synthetic religion. They look like the real thing. They are beautiful for a little time but the heat of problems or demands of standing for the right will cause them to fall by the wayside.

My husband was very disappointed when we had some expensive photographs made. His tie showed up in the picture to be a very odd color. In reality it is a very nice looking tie, a pleasant color, a shade of blue.

"Your tie is made of synthetic material and the film and the synthetic material just didn't work out compatibly."

The picture was made and we could do nothing about the tie.

So it will be in the Great Judgment Morning. Many people who have lived synthetic lives will be revealed in their true colors as they stand before God.

It will be sad but true, they cannot make a change at that time, their opportunity for change will be passed.

A woman of much influence in her city, church, and social circles, lost her husband. He, too, had been popular with the people in their town. He was always a welcome after-dinner speaker.

Everyone rallied around at the time of the man's death. Gifts of food, flowers, and kind deeds flowed in. People felt the widow would set a fine Christian example in her great sorrow.

She missed her opportunity completely. Each day she drove out to the cemetery and spent much time shedding tears. Never once did she testify that she knew her loved one to be in Heaven. It was as if she had completely forgotten God.

People began to say, "Can it be she does not really know God?"

One man who had been very close to the couple was heard to say, "I guess they had synthetic religion."

The widow was left well off financially. She could have gone back to her place in the community and accomplished much good. I am sorry to say she never did. In a few months her friends stopped going to her home and she gradually became a bitter recluse.

No one wants to be a synthetic person. Everyone likes a person who is genuine and true. We can only be real and honest by serving one master, the Lord Jesus Christ.

In New Mexico there are low places called arroyos. In the dry season these places look harmless enough. People drive cars across them. Some foolish people have been known to put up tents and spend the night in an arroyo. When spring comes and the snow in the mountains begins to melt the arroyos are very dangerous. People have lost their lives while trying to drive across some of them. The water comes down in a flood and catches them before they can get to higher ground.

Many people who are synthetic Christians really think they will someday commit their lives to Christ and make a change. Most of them are caught unaware by the flood of life and it is too late to make a change.

The person who pretends to be serving Christ while in his heart he is serving mammon, often does a great harm to those under his influence.

I once knew a young woman whose dressmaker called her an imitation person. The dressmaker knew that the girl had pads built into her clothes to make her look like a nice normal healthy girl. In truth she was very thin and frail. When she married her husband was disappointed in her, not just her physical make up but her attitudes and habits were far from what he had thought. Their marriage only lasted a short while. Synthetic actions come to light all too often after marriage.

There can be no real happiness and joy in a life lived in a make-believe fashion. We must be real to be satisfied with ourselves.

Happiness

Now happiness is in the way that you think,
And not in your food, nor the things that you drink;
It's not in the style of the clothes that you wear,
Nor yet in the cut nor the length of your hair.

It's not in the speed that you go on your way,
Nor the number of things that you do every day;
It's not in abundance of money or mink,
But happiness is in the way that you think.

Synthetic Religion

Now selfishness leads ofttimes into crime,
And greed robs the life of its joy every time;
    But peace in the heart puts you on heaven's brink,
    For happiness is in the way that you think.
                        — J. T. Bolding

13

Fixed Annuities

"And I give unto them eternal life; and they shall never perish, neither shall any man pluck them out of my hand."
— John 10:28

A fixed annuity is primarily an investment to build a retirement income. There are different ways these annuities may be purchased.

I know several school teachers who have a certain amount deducted from their salaries each month and placed into an annuity fund. When you buy an annuity you are usually furnishing money for a company to invest for you. A company can often make better investments than a private individual because of the larger buying power.

You may never own even a dollar's worth of annuity stock. Yet you have something far greater to invest, something that will in your declining years pay you great dividends. Your life invested for Christ will not return to you empty.

We hear lots said about tax advantages of this or that annuity.

Invest your life in Christian service. There will be no tax advantage, except for the deduction of your gifts from your Income Tax. Yet I want to urge you to see the advantages of a home paid for, Heavenly home. The advantages of never having a sorrow or grief. Never being hungry or thirsty, never in pain or trouble.

And God shall wipe away all tears from their eyes; and there shall be no more death, neither sorrow, nor crying, neither shall there be any more pain: for the former things are passed away (Rev. 21:4).

Have you ever read an insurance policy that sounded as wonderful as the verse above? Have you heard of a stock that offered as much?

Often people say, "I want to buy some stock I can see returns on immediately."

Any investment you make in living a life for Christ will pay dividends any day you are in need and bow down to pray and ask for help.

A woman grown old and placed by her children in a nursing home, was often lonely. Then one day a young woman with several children started coming to see her. The young mother brought her children and they sang songs to her.

"Why are you so good to me?" she asked one day. "Your visits are the brightest spot in my week."

"I'm sure you have forgotten a girl named Betty Smith. She was little and ugly and afraid of life. You visited in her home when she was ten and invited her to go to your Sunday School class. I am Betty. You opened a new world to me when you took me to your class."

"Why Betty, I thought you moved away the next year."

"Yes, we were always moving, but I determined to make my life good like yours. I visit to pay you back a little."

The old woman thought a long time after the young mother and her children had gone. She thought of all the girls she had taught through the years. Where are the nine? she asked. "One is enough, just to know I helped one so underfed and neglected as Betty was brings me joy."

So we go day by day investing in our annuity for a better life. At times we feel neglected and alone, then comes one to brighten our day.

I remember one Christmas, I was feeling very blue. It

seemed to me I could not find time to write. I felt helpless and useless. One day in the mail I received a letter from far away, from a woman I had never met.

"Your book brought a blessing to my life," she wrote.

I rushed to the typewriter and my fingers began to fly. A word of encouragement came just when I needed it most.

The people in this world keep trying to buy security and love with money. Security and love can be bought with unselfish trust in Christ and a life lived in His service.

In the early days of the settlement of farms in Northeast Texas a country preacher moved on a small place. He had several children, and a wife who was not too strong.

His crop was growing but the family was very hard pressed for food until the harvest time could come. One day a letter came from a church several miles away, asking the man to come and hold a revival for them.

He went with his wife to the kitchen and they took stock of the food on hand.

"There is just enough to keep you and the children until I return," he told her, "The Lord has called me to go for the meeting, He will provide food when I return."

The revival was good and many people were converted. For some reason no one mentioned an offering and the minister rode his horse home emptyhanded.

The poor wife was beside herself with worry. Some people passing through the country had stopped one day for a meal and she had used part of her meager stores to feed them. The day her husband was to return she had nothing to feed the children.

"Be sweet and don't cry," she told them, "Daddy will be home by noon and he will bring some food."

Soon after noon the minister rode into his front yard. He was so sad. He dreaded telling his wife that the people in the church had not even given him an old-fashioned pounding.

He called his wife and children into the house and they knelt in prayer to ask God for help.

"Dear God you have never failed me and I know my little ones will not have to go hungry all day."

Just as he finished praying a wagon came into the yard. Two men came to the door.

"We heard how your good wife took in some strangers and fed them this week. They were our relatives coming from back east," the men said. "We went around and gathered up some provisions for your family."

The wagon was filled with meat and lard, flour and meal, canned fruit and other things from more settled and prosperous farmers' storehouses. Plenty to run the family until harvest.

The poor minister had never heard of an annuity but he knew where he was investing his life and felt secure in his choice.

On the Death of a Friend

'Tis victory today, at last;
 Our dear friend has achieved;
With sin and sorrow all now past,
 God's call he has received.

This call to happiness and joy,
 Unmarred by grief or pains,
Anticipated since a boy,
 Gives peace that never wanes.

Eternity with God to stay;
 No heartache or remorse;
Eternal, glorious, endless day
 In heaven to rejoice.
    — J. T. Bolding

14

Baggage Men

"But as his part is that goeth down to the battle, so shall his part be that tarrieth by the stuff: they shall part alike." — I Samuel 30:24

In war time with battles going on, there must be some to go and fight and some to remain by the baggage and keep materials and food ready for the fighters. David set the example of sharing with these baggage men in the Old Testament.

In our modern, rushing world, we find there are still many ways people must be trusted to stand by the stuff.

Once we had a little car trouble far out from town. We stopped near an old filling station for several minutes, while getting the car repaired. Having nothing better to do and the sun being too hot to stay in the car I sat in the station.

A huge trailer truck stopped at the pump for gas. The driver was in no hurry at all. He joked about his mileage. He gives no thought to his boss, sitting back in the home office getting ulcers because the trucks do not get through quicker.

In contrast to the slow, easy-going trucker, the next customer was a traveling salesman. He urged everyone in sight to hurry. He is anxious to get out into the stream of traffic and find a place to make more dollars. The world of commerce is out ahead and the salesman plans to conquer it. His wife is at home with the children. She takes care of family problems, he is a salesman.

Everything stops around the busy little station for a moment. The manager suspects one of the hands of failure in collecting for a tank of gas.

The three hands are questioned and reprimanded. I hate to say anything but I did see the customer in question place some money on top of the cash register and hurry away. At last I told the manager to look there. All was settled and they rushed back to work.

The manager began telling me what a time he had with his dumb hands. I had been thinking they worked very hard.

Two ragged little children came in with a few empty pop bottles to sell. Their eyes lit up when the man gave them a few pennies. They were still looking at the candy counter when my husband came to tell me the car was repaired and we could leave.

As we drove happily down the road I thought of the story of King David and his men in battle and by the stuff. Life for everyone is like that. Some must go and work in one way while others must keep the home fires kindled. All in their places are important.

Always there is a need for work, at home, at church, just out in the world at large.

When tax-paying time comes we often think our great country is filled with more people who do not put into the tax funds, but expect to be kept up by them. We grow impatient with such people, we wonder why they can't find some useful work to do.

Our church work is very similar to the truck driver and the salesman and the children.

Some of the members care very little whether the world hears about Jesus. They take life slowly and in fun are at ease. Others are in a mad rush to get things done and feel impatient with those who keep their name on the roll but do not come or get involved.

Then there are many new Christians, like the little children with a few bottles to sell. The timid babe in Christ, longs for the glorious goodies he feels mature Christians possess.

All people are not alike, yet all are involved in life in their own way.

What have we been doing since we gave our hearts to Christ!

Make yourself available to God and He will put you to work. You may be one of the baggagemen left behind to keep the records or even sweep the floor, but you will share in the rewards of glory.

If God had wanted all His children to be and do exactly the same thing he would have cut all from the same pattern.

Many women have a good deal of spare time and spend that time helping out at clinics and mission churches. It can be very depressing for those who cannot find the time to do these extras. But we should not let it "get us down" as the saying goes. We should each take care of our baggage in our own way and be happy in doing it.

God gave every person some baggage to stand by. Not all people are endowed alike. We are responsible for the stuff we are given to stand by, not what our friend or neighbor has.

A young minister grieved because he could not sway the audiences like his friend who was an evangelist. Yet the modest young pastor was greatly beloved by his church people. He was never too tired to rush to a home where death had entered. He visited the sick and gathered up food for the needy. He would never stand before great crowds and feel their praise and acclaim, yet God knew he was doing each day the tasks assigned to him.

Only a Smile?

It was only a smile that he gave me,
    As we each went his own busy way,

But it helped me to face life more bravely,
  And my outlook was brighter that day.

It was only a smile that he gave me,
  But to me it was wondrous indeed:
It restored ebbing hopes e'er so quickly,
  And full filled my poor heart's crying need.
                              — J. T. Bolding

Some sage made this statement: The man who holds the ladder firmly at the bottom is about as important as the man at the top.

15

Valuable Things—Friends

"A friend loveth at all times." — Proverbs 17:17
*"And the scripture was fulfilled which saith, Abraham
believed God, and it was imputed unto him for righteousness: and he was called the friend of God."*
                                                    — James 2:23

A person is truly wealthy if he has a true friend.

What is a friend? Not just someone you happen to be
acquainted with. Not just someone you went to school with
as a child. A true friend is different.

The Bible says Abraham was a friend of God. What did
this friendship show? Two communing together. God told
Abraham of His great dreams and plans for a chosen people.
He promised Abraham a part in those dreams and plans.
Abraham on the other side worshiped God and tried to obey
his commands. He loved God to such an extent he was
willing to sacrifice his only son, when God gave the command.

We want a friend who likes us just as we are; one who
is proud of our successes and sad at our failures. A real
friend will not be jealous. A real friend will think of your
best interest first and his own second.

On a very cold winter's day in 1874 a boy from Hungary,
landed in New York. As he stood shivering in the immigration
office, he was thinking of the great opportunities in the great

land of America. The officer in charge looked at the fifteen
year old boy with interest.

"Do you have money to live on until you find work?" he
asked.

"No sir, I have only five cents left," the boy replied.

"I am sorry son but it is a rule that an immigrant must
have some money to live on."

"Are there no other rules?" the trembling boy asked.

"Well, yes, if you have friends in America who would
look after you, I could let you enter."

"Oh, sir, that is no problem. I am close friends with
three Americans."

"Wonderful, who are they?"

"Ben Franklin, Abraham Lincoln, and Harriet Beecher
Stowe," the boy proudly replied.

The officer knew the boy could only know the three great
people from the books he read.

"I believe I will take a chance on a boy with friends such
as these."

Michael Pupin was allowed to enter the United States. He
worked and educated himself at Columbia University. He
became a college teacher and contributed much to America
in his advancement of electro-mechanics. He was able to do
this because he had the right friends as a boy.

Before the age of television many children and adults
found their best friends in books.

All Christians must have some close friends between the
pages of the Bible. When we are in trouble we often think
of dear Job. When in love we remember Ruth. When we
want an example of courage we have only to think of the
beautiful Esther. What better friends could we find anyplace?

We must meet often with our friends in the Bible. They
will never gossip, nor tell our shared secrets. We can pattern
our lives after them and find fulfilment and happiness.

A gift of friendship bestowed on others is like a piece of

bread cast upon the water, it will come back to you many times over when you need it most.

A man was known for always helping other people. He made his livelihood working a farm. Often he would take a day off from his own work to help a friend catch up. His wife often complained and said he was unappreciated. Then the good neighbor broke his leg in an accident.

The wife was bitter and felt he was being punished for something.

As the wife looked out each day at the cotton fields, ready for harvest, and no one to gather it, she was bitter.

Then one morning as her husband was making his way painfully, on crutches, back from feeding the livestock, something happened.

A long line of cotton pickers began coming up the road and into the fields. A group of women drove up in cars and began taking out food for a noon meal.

With a dozen mechanical harvesters in the field, the cotton was all harvested by the middle of the afternoon.

"How can I ever thank you?" the farmer said, with tears of gratitude in his eyes.

It has always been a tradition and practice in America for friends to help in time of illness. Good friends are like umbrellas in the rain, they help shelter us from the storm.

Christians have many friends we will never see or know personally. We have friends in the people we help in foreign lands. Our mission money goes to tell others of a friend who is always kind and forgiving. We will never see these people but we are their friends if we help them to hear the gospel.

Never say you have no calling in life. Every person is called to be a friend. Develop your talent for friendship.

You

You've been such a dear friend
To me for so long;

You've brought me true gladness,
    My heart's known a song.
You've been where I needed
    You — Friendship I've tried;
You've shared in my joys, in
    My sorrows you've cried.

I wish I had words to
    Express how I care,
I want you to know that
    You're e'er in my prayer.
I hope that for long I
    May share in your day —
I love to be near you
    At work or in play.
                    — Jewel Alice McLeod

16

One in a Multitude

"But when he saw the multitudes, he was moved with compassion on them, because they fainted and were scattered abroad, as sheep having no shepherd."
— Matthew 9:36

Last year we drove along the coast line from San Diego, California to El Segundo, California. There are many towns along the route. We were amazed at all the young people we saw standing on corners, walking along the streets, and a few in cars. They were so different from the youth we were accustomed to seeing in our own home town in Texas.

The day was very cool and most of the youth had on some type of coat, jacket or blanket. Many were barefoot or wearing only sandals. Most looked hungry and dirty. Their hair was so long we had to look close to tell the girls from the boys.

I think I understood that day just a little of what our Saviour meant when he was moved with compassion at the sight of the multitude.

We thought of our own precious teen-age grandchildren and how clean and fresh they always try to look. Then we thought of a dear niece who had gone with a friend to Europe, alone. Our hearts felt sad as we could see how she might be dirty, tired, hungry, wandering over a foreign land.

My heart cried out: "Oh, dear Father in Heaven, what have we done to these poor, lost children?"

Christ had a compassionate heart because he was concerned about the needs of the multitude. When He saw them hungry He wanted to and did feed them. When He saw the multitude sick, or dying He healed them.

To understand the compassionate heart of Christ, we must have a concern for those we rub shoulders with in the multitude.

Every person wants to be loved, to be recognized, to be appreciated. We seek these three things in different ways. Many small children try getting attention by having tantrums. We have a generation of teen-agers seeking recognition by going against the regular pattern set by their elders.

Man has a capacity for loving others, but for that love to be like Christ's love it must be centered on others, not on self.

Often we read articles which tell us the earth will be so filled with people in the next hundred years, there will be no room and no food for the multitudes.

You have to admit that we live in a day when there are multitudes all about us. How easy it is to say, "I am only one in a crowd, what can I do?"

All great inventions, movements, discoveries, are started first in the mind of one person. That one person inspires someone else with his thoughts or ideas and something big is developed.

Christ was one man, in a multitude, yet he started a kingdom that will not cease to grow until the end of the world.

When Christ looked at the multitudes He saw people distressed, harrassed, helpless. He wanted to help them.

What do people see in the multitudes today? A politician sees votes, a merchant sees customers, a doctor sees patients, an actor sees an audience. What do we as Christians see in the multitude? Do we see poor people who make our taxes higher because they must have welfare? Do we see criminals who keep us afraid at night? Do we see those who would make the world more beautiful and good?

I read a story in the newspaper about a Judge in the great city of Chicago who saw a wild Negro boy standing before him to be sent to a prison with hardened criminals. The Judge felt the boy had a capacity for leadership if he could only get a glimpse of the better things in life. He sent the boy, instead of to prison, to a place far across the city where a trusted man took charge of him. Under the kind treatment and love of the Christian man, this boy learned to know Christ. He went to school and in no way disappointed the Judge.

I knew a High School teacher who looked in the multitude of students for one real scholar. When he found one he made every effort to help him make the most of his mind and opportunities.

In the midst of the multitude are we trying to pass by without looking at the needs we might be able to meet?

You are one in a multitude, yet you can be faithful to the things entrusted to your care. You can be friendly to those who are not easy to like. You can try to dispel gloom and fear. You can work at honest toil.

One can have a far reaching influence for good or bad. A boy once thought it would be funny if he cried out, "Fire."

A large group of people were eating in a restaurant when the boy tried his experiment. At the word fire, they rushed for the door. Many ran out without their coats and purses. The foolish boy sat drinking his coke and laughing.

The police had a way, when the manager called them, of making the boy see what a serious offense he had committed.

A faithful teacher in a High School wanted to form an organization that would appeal to all the boys and girls in a large school. She announced a meeting time for all to come who wanted to belong to an exclusive organization.

She was pleased when a large group came to the first

meeting. She organized the group with officers, then she appointed a program committee. This organization met early before school and the programs were put on by the students themselves. The programs were different from regular chapel meetings, in that they were religious. No set doctrine was taught, no sermons were preached, but there was an outlet for good musicians, good speakers, good leaders. All because one teacher saw a need in the multitude of students.

One in a multitude can do much harm or accomplish much good. Only that one can make the choice.

> Grant me, O Lord, the strength today
> For every task which comes my way.
> Cover my eyes and make me blind
> To petty faults I should not find.
> Open my eyes and let me see
> The friend my neighbor tries to be.
> Teach me, when duty seems severe,
> To see my purpose shining clear.
> Let me at noontime rest content
> The half-day bravely lived and spent.
> And when the night slips down, let me
> Unstained and undishonored be.
> Grant me to live this one day through
> Up to the best that I can do.
> — Author unknown

17

A Hole in Your Pocket

"For to him that is joined to all the living there is hope: for a living dog is better than a dead lion. For the living know that they shall die." — Ecclesiastes 9:4, 5

As a small child I watched, fascinated, as my mother made miniature aprons. Each apron had a small pocket.

"We will give each lady in the church an apron and ask her to fill the pocket with change," she explained to me. "Then we will take all the change and give it to our mission offering."

When my mother left the machine to go to the kitchen I undertook to make an apron for myself. When I thought my apron was finished I went to my secret bank and took out my small hoard of pennies.

After I placed my pennies in the pocket I started for the kitchen to show my mother. By the time I reached the kitchen only one penny remained in the pocket.

"You have a hole in your pocket," Mother said. "You forgot to sew one side."

I spent several moments trying to find my lost pennies.

God gives to each person a pocketful of days at birth. As children we do not notice that our pocket leaks. We just live each day as it comes. We are more excited at one time than another as when we are awaiting Christmas or Thanksgiving.

When we trust Christ as our Saviour we feel an urge to spend our days serving Him. Life is precious and sweet to the Christian. As knowledge that our days are going swiftly dawns on us, we want to make each day count for good.

Isaiah 55:1 becomes a favorite verse with us. We want every one to come to know of the living waters. but the pocket filled with days gradually grows more and more empty.

Where we once were too busy to notice the passing of the days, now we find them going all too quickly as we grow older.

Too often in place of saying, "Lord what wilt Thou have me to do?" we try not to notice that there are things to be done.

Our worst enemy is ourselves. We realize our days are going quickly. Often we grow selfish and think of the things we still want to experience and do before our pocket of days is completely empty.

There was a couple who spent their time and money making one long trip after another. When they came home they were dissatisfied and started planning another trip.

Friends who have visited Australia tell me of a plant, called the Nardoo plant. The natives eat this plant and feel full, but it has no food value, their body suffers for nutritious food.

Lean souls die hungry. They seek the selfish things on which to spend their precious days.

So we know that every person has a pocket of days. Some more than others. But each person is responsible for the way they spend their days. As a child I could go back and search for my lost pennies and put them back in a safe place. As an adult there is no way you can find the days you have lost, they are gone. So it is important to think each day of the good you can do, not the past or the future but the day in your hand.

A man and his wife wanted to find a useful project for

their retirement years. One day as they looked at some lots they owned in a very poor part of town they had an inspiration.

"Look at the children playing in the street," the man said. "Why don't we turn our lots into a playground for them?"

The couple spent money and time on the playground. Each day found them there sitting on a bench. The children soon began to talk to them, to tell of their problems. The man and his wife talked to the ones in need, they encouraged them to stay in school. For a number of years they went each day to the playground to be with "their children" as they called the ones who came to the park. The hole in their pocket of days grew larger and at last there were no more days. Many people mourned at their deaths. Many children, almost grown, thanked God for the help they had received at the playground.

When the Young Are Grown

Once the house was lovely,
But it's lonely here today,
For time has come and stained its walls
An' called the young away;
An' all that's left for mother
An' for me till life is through
Is to sit an' tell each other
What the children used to do.

We couldn't keep 'em always,
An' we knew it from the start;
We knew when they were babies,
That some day we'd have to part.
But the years go by so swiftly,
An' the littlest one has flown,
An' there's only me an' mother
Now left here to live alone.

Oh, there's just one consolation,
As we're sitting here at night,
They've grown to men and women,
An' we've brought 'em up alright;
We've watched 'em as we've loved 'em

> An' they're splendid, every one,
> An' we feel the Lord won't blame us
> For the way our work was done.
>
> They're clean, an' kind, an' honest,
> An' the world respects 'em, too;
> That's the dream of parents always,
> An 'our dreams have all come true.
> So although the house is lonely,
> An' sometimes our eyes grow wet,
> We are proud of them an' happy,
> An' we've nothing to regret.
> — Author Unknown

God rains goodness and mercy upon the days as they drop from our pocket. It is up to each of us how we sow and cultivate, so that the rains may help to produce fruit.

18

Leftover Heaven

"We give thanks to God and the Father of our Lord Jesus Christ, praying always for you, since we heard of your faith in Christ Jesus, and of the love which ye have to all the saints, for the hope which is laid up for you in heaven. . . ." — Colossians 1:3, 4, 5

"The last shall be first, and the first last: for many be called, but few chosen." — Matthew 20:16

My father was a minister for two rural churches while I was going through the hungry stage. If you have ever watched a teen-ager growing up you will remember that stage. They get up from the table walk to the door and back and ask for something else to eat.

Now I know the cooks in my father's churches were the greatest, but as hostesses they fell short of my expectations. The adults were always seated at the dining table and the children had to wait until they finished. We had the leftovers to eat. Well, sometimes, by the time we had waited an hour those leftovers were just like eating bits of heavenly hash.

There are so many times in our life as adults when we feel we have had to wait for the good things in life. When our turn comes isn't it just like having a bit of leftover heaven.

A dear lady I knew in one of my husband's churches told me about her leftover experiences.

She was the mother of three boys. She brought them up in a three-room house. She knew her husband owned several good farms. She also knew he gave generously to the church. She never had thought to ask for a larger, better house until her oldest son was sixteen. He happened to read in a denominational paper about his father giving a large sum of money to a denominational university for a scholarship fund. That evening at dinner he told his father a few things about charity beginning at home.

The father was really a good man but he just thought of other things before his family.

"Well, son, if that is the way it looks to you," the man told his son, "you and your mother go into town and buy a nice home, we must live in the village for you boys to attend high school. Let her get what she wants."

My friend told me how happy she and her three boys were as they looked at houses, they all seemed beautiful to her because she had lived crowded so many years. They found just what the boys liked, three bedrooms upstairs and two downstairs. The kitchen was big and had lots of cabinet space.

"My heaven was late coming, but it has been so wonderful all these years," she would beam proudly at her home. "Also the scholarship my husband gave has helped our grandchildren attend college."

Often when we are middle aged we feel only the leftovers of life are ours. That is not true at all. We no longer are able to excel at sports, or academic matters. We may not be able to go out and work for wages or just go out and shop all day. Think of all the things one has to be thankful and happy for in those leftover years of life.

'Tis true your family is grown and gone from home. 'Tis true you may no longer need to work for money. Think of all the wonderful things you can do with the time you now have to call your own.

There are so many good books to be read, so many kinds of handwork to engage in, even so many shows and musicals to enjoy.

I heard a lady say, "I have lived all my life for others, now I will do just as I please and please only myself."

She had the wrong outlook. The leftover years can really bring heaven nearer if we put them to good use. Some outstanding people have been successful as artists, writers, even inventors, after the middle of life was passed.

Then, most important of all, there is time in the late years to serve our Master. There are always people who need to hear about Christ; always people who need words of comfort for their sad hearts.

My friend Mollie bought and planted a pecan tree on her seventieth birthday. Why?

"I want to leave something growing for others to enjoy long after I am gone to heaven."

Leftovers can be very good. It is all in the way we look at them. But you must do your own looking.

When my children were little and people in our vicinity still baked biscuits every day, I often had some bread left over from breakfast. My, what a wonderful dessert I would make out of those cold biscuits. Mixed with eggs and milk, sugar and nutmeg, they turned into the greatest puddings. The children never complained that their pudding was made from leftovers. They just enjoyed eating the pudding.

People are not standing around waiting to complain that you are too old to tell them about Christ. They are often wishing they had some of the grace and fortitude you seem to possess. You are the one who makes yourself a leftover when you fail to do your best to make life full and happy.

Browning wrote:

> Grow old along with me!
> The best is yet to be,

The last of life, for which the
first was made:
Our times are in his hand
Who saith, "A whole I planned,
Youth shows but half; trust God:
see all, nor be afraid."

Leftovers

As a boy, our old clock once stopped running,
And my father allowed me to clean it;
I was faced by a fact that was stunning
In the leftover parts, and I mean it!

When our car seemed to need some attention,
And I tried, by myself, to repair it,
There were leftover parts I won't mention
And my care only seemed to impair it.

All these leftovers seemed mine to care for;
It was my job to get them in place;
As a workman 'twas mine to prepare for
Their replacement if I saved my face.

My dear wife, having served a big dinner,
Has her problems it's not hard to see,
But she tells me that I am the winner
As she feeds her leftovers to me.

— J. T. Bolding

19

He Knows Your Name

"And these are the names of the men." — Numbers 1:5

A large part of the book of Numbers is spent counting and numbering people.

Why?

Because God knows his people individually. He knows what they stand for and how they spend their time and efforts.

A small child, near Christmastime became worried. He was afraid Santa Claus would not know his name and he would not get the gifts he so very much wanted. His mother had been very patient with him, writing letters and taking him to see all kinds of fake Santas in department stores.

"How will he know when he gets to our house?" the little one asked.

The mother made a large felt boot and across the top she pasted in contrasting colors the letters TEDDY.

The child was delighted and settled down to wait for the eventful coming of his toys.

I have known people who said they were Christians. They said they had given their hearts to Christ, yet they were constantly bothered with the questions, Does He know my name? Does He know where I live? Will He take me to heaven?

Yes, if you are His child He knows your name and it is written in the book of life.

In 1968 I flew to the city of St. Louis, all alone. I felt as if I had completely lost my identity. I saw no one on the plane I knew. When I changed planes, I was pushed aside for others more important and only at the last moment was given a seat.

Then I arrived in the big city, big for a woman from a West Texas town. A limousine took me from the airport to a large hotel.

When the uniformed doorman picked up my luggage and took me inside, my first impression was, Where did all these people come from?

I was as lost as a little flea on the back of a prize poodle.

At the admitting desk I took a card from my purse and presented it to the man in charge. The card had been sent to me by my publishers, I was to be their guest that week.

Suddenly I wasn't a little lost flea any more, I was Amy Bolding, a guest of a big publishing house. People were busy taking me to a beautiful suite of rooms. Everything was for my comfort and enjoyment.

I had never met the men from the publishing company, but they knew me through my books.

As God's children we have a distinct advantage. He knows our names, He knows our works and we do not have to present a card for Him to know who we are.

When my son was a small boy, the family called him Sonny. One day as he played in the front yard a strange man walked by. As he passed he spoke to my son: "Hello Sonny." The child rushed into the house all excited: "Mother, that man knew my name."

Does it excite you to know God knows your name? It is a serious thought to know that God knows our name and expects us to live up to our abilities.

An unknown writer put it this way:

The past is settled, the future is secure;

Therefore for the present,
Walk lighter,
Look brighter,
Gird up tighter,
For the Father himself loveth us.

Not only does a parent know the name of his child, he usually knows why he gave that child a certain name. He knows the good traits and the bad of his child. A child may be able to fool an earthly parent at times. A child of God can hide nothing from him.

The next time you feel you are a nonenity, try stopping to remember God knows your name.

Many people know your name. When they hear your name, what do they think?

A man living in a city of ten thousand people, was well known as a bootlegger. He made money, lived in a fairly nice house for that city. His daughter was not able to make any nice friends in school. Everyone knew her father's name and it stood for something evil and bad.

Being young and wanting to have a good time the girl gave her affections too lavishly to the boys in her school. As was to be expected she became the mother of an illegitimate child.

This poor child was under a double cloud, the ugly name of an unlawful grandfather and the disgraced name of her unwed mother. The girl was beautiful and had a brilliant mind.

When she finished high school she asked her grandparents to send her away to college. Far away where her name was not known she made a success of her life. One day some people happened to visit in the city where the girl was teaching school. They were not nice enough to keep quiet. They told about the young woman's grandfather and mother. Little whispers became rumors and at the end of the term she was asked to leave her position.

When we have a bad name we not only suffer ourselves but we cause innocent people to suffer.

A name is a precious gift to be guarded well, to be made known as representing someone good and true.

My Name

I met a man the other day;
 He called me by my name;
With glowing heart I went my way
 Refreshed for life's hard game.

Real friends will love us as we are:
 Although we have no fame
They'll recognize us from afar
 And call us by our name.

It is a joy to me to know
 God's Son to earth once came
To save my sinful soul, and so
 I'm glad He knows my name.
      — J. T. Bolding

20

Between the Fences

"Thou wilt keep him in perfect peace, whose mind is stayed on thee: because he trusteth in thee." — Isaiah 23:3

A family living on a farm in Northeast Texas had trouble getting their cows and horses back and forth to the pasture because they wanted to stop and wander out into the fields on the way.

When the boys in the family began to grow older and have ideas they asked their father to buy some wire and posts. They put up a fence on each side of the path leading across the fields to the pasture on the back side of the farm. After that each morning they opened the gate and started the livestock down the path. The fence on either side kept them out of the fields. The boys were never late to school again because they had to take the cows to pasture.

When we are born we enter a fenced area. The fence on one side is birth and the one on the other side is death. All the days of our lives we stay between the two fences.

We know the date the birth occurred but we have no way of knowing when we will come to the fence that says, The End.

Some fellows stay right in the rut
While others head the throng.
All men may be born equal but —

> They don't stay that way long.
> There is many a man with a gallant air,
>   Goes galloping to the fray;
> But the valuable man is the man who's there
>   When the smoke has cleared away.
> Some "don't get nuthin' out of life"
>   But when their whines begin,
> We often can remind them that
>   They "don't put nothin' in."
>   — Author Unknown

Once an employer was disturbed because a worker always came late to work. "Don't you know what time we start work in this store?" he asked.

"No, sir, they are always at work when I get here, I don't know when they start."

Many people treat life like that tardy employee. We know life is going when we become aware of it and we make little effort to catch up.

The farm boys went to school feeling sure and safe because they trusted their fence to guide the cattle to the pasture. Many a working woman goes to work feeling secure about her home because she leaves a trusted servant or loved one to take care of things at home.

Christ went back to his heavenly home because His work on earth was finished, He left it in the hands of His trusted followers. We claim to be those followers. Are we living up to the trust placed in us?

We are born between two fences, we can never go back to the first fence, we are constantly getting closer to the last fence. As we go along the way between the fences we must be sure to gather every morsel for good and happiness we can find. "The fruit of the Spirit is love, joy, peace, long-suffering, gentleness, goodness, faith" (Gal. 5:22).

If we are saved individuals we find the fruits spoken of all along the way. Some people like us to think they are great producers of the fruit of the Spirit. Their lives tell

81

on them. In our human strength we can produce no fruit, we must be living in the Spirit.

When we are born we have sin in our hearts. It is there and we have no say about it. Sin rises from within.

When we reach the age of accountability, if we give our hearts to Christ, we try to keep sin out of our lives and hearts. We cannot wholly succeed at this. Yet the verse at the beginning of this chapter tells us how we may live in trust and faith.

Have you ever made a trip and watched for some signpost along the way? Someone asks you to come for a visit and they tell you to turn at a certain corner. You follow their instructions and you arrive safely.

There are some sign posts we have along our way, the way we treat those with whom we live; the way we give to those in need; the way we attend our chosen church; the way we read the guide book, our Bible.

As we go along between these two fences we are not without a guide post. Our parents have often pointed out a better way for us to travel, our friends have given us advice, we have the example of others we can see.

In spite of all the examples and advice we always must remember we are first, last, and always, accountable to God for the way we use the time given us.

We do not want to be like the teacher who went to school in a bad frame of mind. His wife had been angry with him and he was discouraged.

"I wonder if my life is really worth living!" he exclaimed to his first class.

"Well sir," a bright pupil remarked, "what else can you do with it?"

There are so many wonderful things to do with the life we have between the fence of birth and the fence of death, we must not waste any of it complaining, finding fault, or being unkind.

A young woman found herself in the position of an older

daughter, in a home where the mother was frail and there were six younger children. As the years passed she saw her sisters married and in homes of their own. Her brothers left to become successful business men. She always seemed to be the one left to do the work at home. The few young men that had been around married someone else. Then her mother lost her eye sight. The girl was now a woman and there was no way to leave home.

It often seemed to her she was fenced in and tied to her parents. But she always was kind and patient with them.

After the blind mother died she asked her father to give her enough money to take a trip.

"No, you stay and cook for me, you can take a trip when I am gone."

She was disappointed but went on taking care of the home and saying little. Her father did buy her a car so she could go about town easier.

After a few years, the father also died. The brothers and sisters gathered in to hear the will read. They knew their father was as we say in Texas, "well fixed."

Each one received a few thousand dollars. The bulk of his property and money went to the daughter who had so sweetly and kindly cared for him and his wife for the best years of her life.

She felt as if she could fly. Life had been so trying. Now she was rich. She could do anything she pleased. With a school day friend, who like herself, had been tied down for many years, she took the trip about which she had dreamed.

Often we think we are being forced along in a path we do not want to take, then suddenly there is a great reward.

Remember the Rich Young Ruler in the Bible. He had lived what he considered to be a good life, yet he lacked something. We cannot be good enough in our own strength to open the gate which reads, "Eternal Life in Heaven." When we come to that last fence, if we have given our hearts to Christ, He will be there to open the gate and say, "Well done."

Patience

No finer grace for old or young
Than bridle for impulsive tongue —
    The choice of the gentle line,
When provocation's smarting bite
Injury brings, and 'twould seem right
    To retaliate in kind.

It takes a man of strength to wait,
Withhold the fiery darts of hate,
    To reply in gentle tone:
But he who bends the natural turn,
Tho inwardly the soul may burn,
    Has conquered not self alone.

For this exalted, noble part —
A greater thing: A work of art —
    Bi-product of self-control —
Has stamped itself into the life
Of him who was the source of strife,
    Pointing out the better role.

Thru noble ways — examples fine —
We set the pace and draw the line
    To love's everlasting star;
And thus we leave along our way
By what we do — not what we say —
    Sure proof of the men we are.
           — Edward V. Woods

21

Take Christmas with You

"Where is He that is born King of the Jews? For we have seen his star in the east and are come to worship him." — Matthew 2:2

Tom and Mary were having a farewell dinner with their relatives. The next day they, with their small daughters, six and eight years old, would be leaving for a mission assignment in Africa.

The family tried to be happy. They were proud of Tom and Mary, but at times there crept in a sad note.

"We will miss the children so much at Christmas," Tom's mother lamented.

"Better take Christmas with you," an older brother advised and his voice was unnecessarily husky.

It seemed to Tom and Mary that the whole town waited at the station to tell them goodbye. Relatives from near and far were all around. Both grandmothers took their turns loving the little girls, and the grandfathers filled their pockets with nickels and dimes to be spent on the boat.

The train arrived, the little family waved out the windows until they were out of sight. Exhausted they settled down to relax and enjoy the ride.

"Mommie, did God also call Sue and me to Africa?" Jennifer asked, as they were speeding across the country side.

"Yes, dear, He called you because you belong to us," Mary replied. "And I am afraid you will be the ones to make the greatest sacrifices."

"What is a sacrifice?" Sue asked.

"Mother means you will not have a nice school to attend," Tom explained. "She will be your teacher."

The train ride was exciting. The ocean liner they traveled on was more fun than the family ever dreamed about.

They had to stay a week with a mission family in the port city before they could find a way to take their many pieces of luggage and few pieces of furniture to their mission station a hundred miles inland.

Once at their station they settled down to a new way of life. There were many new things to learn, many strange people with whom to make friends.

They scarcely noticed being in a strange land for the Thanksgiving time. The day Mary tore off the month of November from the calendar, the girls became excited. There in big, bold, red letters was December 25. Their thoughts became filled with Christmas.

The two children began to worry. Would they have a Christmas tree? Where could they get one? All the trees were very tall and they were the wrong kind.

"We will have to think of a different tree this year," Mary told them. "We may not have any gifts to put under a tree."

The two children could not help being sad and homesick. They wanted Christmas at Grandmother's house, as they had always known it.

The mail did not come often to their mission station and the whole family felt that gifts from home might not arrive in time. Mary managed to make some candy, and fruit was plentiful.

A few days before Christmas their thoughts were directed away from gifts and happy family times. Tom found four little children whose parents had drowned. No one in the village would take the children into their home. Tom brought them to Mary.

"Find some of your dresses to share with the little girls," Mary told her own children. "We will have to buy some boy's clothes."

The whole family became so involved in taking care of the orphans they almost, but not quite, forgot Christmas.

"Mother even if we have no gifts, we can read the story from the Bible," Jennifer said.

"We can sing the songs we know also," Sue said.

"Oh, that will be great," Mary told the children. "We must find something to give our new children, also."

After the gay and happy program, put on by the missionaries, Mary served candy and fruit, then she put all the children to bed.

When she came back into the living room, tears were flowing freely from her eyes. "Tom I am so homesick, I just can't stand it."

"I don't feel very gay myself," Tom told her, "but we know God called us here, He will help us be brave."

"Why couldn't the mail at least come in time for us to hear from home?"

"Trying to plan and pack for three years I just didn't realize we wouldn't be close to a toy shop," Mary lamented.

As her tears started afresh and Tom almost in tears was trying to comfort her, there came a light tap on the door.

When Tom opened the door there stood a man from the government office.

"I had to come out here on business," he told them, and so I picked up your mail and brought it along."

Mary dried her tears and welcomed their guest into the house.

He handed them a large packet tied with string. One could tell they were Christmas cards.

"Didn't we have any packages?" Mary asked timidly.

"Yes you did," he said, "but I had to ride a motorbike and just couldn't bring them."

"It is our first time to be away from our folks at Christmas," Tom told him. "We are pretty homesick."

"That is why I made an effort to go by and collect your letters," their guest told them. "You may send some back when I leave tomorrow."

A cot was set up in the kitchen for the guest and Tom and Mary sat alone at last to read their letters.

One from both their parents but none of them mentioned Christmas or gifts. Mary began to cry softly again.

"Please don't cry, I can't stand it if you do," Tom pleaded. "Look, here is one from my big brother. Let's read it."

Dear Kids:

I know you were in the clouds so much when you were getting ready, you forgot about Christmas. When we were packing the boxes to be opened for clothes and linens next year, we packed one special one. Look wherever you stored things for future use and open the box labeled, "Packed By Your Big Brother."

Have a merry time, we miss you.

Jack

"Where is that box?" Tom asked.

"I put the boxes for future use under our bed to save space," Mary said.

Soon they were on hands and knees pulling and tugging at boxes until they found the right one.

There right on the top in the box, was an artificial tree. There were all kinds of boxes wrapped and labeled, from both sides of the family.

"How they must have worked to fix all this when we were not looking," Mary marveled.

"Look at this last box!" Tom exclaimed. "It says, 'For the ones you will probably have taken in by this time.' "

Jennifer and Sue did not hurry to get up next morning, they did not want to think about what day it was.

"Well, Sue, we must get up and help take care of the little orphans. After all God called us to come to Africa with mommie and daddy."

"Sue, Jennifer, come quick," Mother called.

"Quick!" Tom urged.

At the door to the living room both girls stopped. There in the corner was a beautiful, little, Christmas tree. Piled all around it were gifts in beautiful packages. On the floor, their eyes bright with expectancy, sat the four little orphans.

"Oh, mommie, a miracle," Sue screamed.

"Yes, we brought Christmas with us and didn't know it."

Mr. Bangcock, the one who brought the mail, spoke but no one heard him, "I believe these Christians always take Christmas with them."

God calls us to go to certain places, He calls us to be still at times, He calls us to return. Wherever our lot may be we need to learn to trust in His providence and care. He knows our needs long before we know them. He has an answer ready for us. I think the little girls remembered the most important part of Christmas when they asked for the Christmas story to be read. We can always worship, we do not need a lot of expensive gifts to remember Christ's birthday and to worship him.

22

Easter Story

*"For thou wilt not leave my soul in hell; neither wilt
thou suffer thine Holy One to see corruption. Thou wilt
show me the path of life: in thy presence is fullness of
joy; at thy right hand there are pleasures for evermore.*
— Psalm 16:10, 11

Pattie met Prince in High School. From the first day in
class together, they were very much attracted to each other.
Pattie's people were not church-going people but to be with
Prince more she started going to his church.

Against the wishes and advice of parents on both sides
they married as soon as they graduated from High School.

The next four years were blissful. Pattie worked all the
time. Prince worked part time and went to college. The
world was bright for them and they were pleased when a
little baby came to bless their home.

Prince was faithful to his church and prayed often that
Pattie would trust Christ and have the full joy of salvation
that he knew.

"Going is enough for me. I'm not too strong on belief in
God," Pattie would say flippantly.

The day came when Pattie needed the strength only a
Christian can have. Prince received orders to report for mili-

tary duty. Only a few more months and he would have been past the age limit, but now he must go.

"It isn't fair," Pattie cried. "You can't go and leave us. What will we do?"

"Well, all things work out for good to them that love the Lord," Prince told her. "I wish you could trust God and feel that He will take care of you."

"I can't believe there is a God who would be so cruel."

"Promise me one thing," Prince demanded. "While I am gone, will you take Lisa every Sunday, unless she is ill."

"You mean to Sunday School?"

"Yes, I mean to Sunday School," Prince was very sincere. "I know my parents will pray for me and will help you in taking care of her. They love you, Pattie."

For a few months Pattie and Lisa lived near the base where Prince was stationed. Then the day came when he had to say good-bye and go to Vietnam.

Since Pattie had a good position in the city where they were living, she stayed on rather than go back to their home town.

Each Sunday she tried to keep her promise by taking Lisa to Sunday School. Her own heart grew more and more cold and bitter.

A man in the office where Pattie worked began to pay much attention to her. On several occasions he asked her for a date.

"No, I am married," she would tell him.

"How long will I have the strength to tell him, no?" she asked herself.

One day a letter came from Prince saying he would be sent home in three more months. He pictured all the good times they would have starting life together all over again. At the close of the letter he wrote: "Lisa, God is over here taking care of me, just like He is there taking care of you."

Pattie still denying she believed in God, breathed an unconscious prayer, "God, if you are here, you better help me, for I am too lonely to be good much longer."

God answered her prayer by having the man who was tempting her transferred to a distant city. The same day the tempter left, Pattie received word that Prince had been wounded in battle.

Picking up Lisa from the nursery school and going to the apartment was a mammoth task as she fought to keep back the tears.

A long distance call to talk to Prince's parents helped some.

"We are constantly in prayer for all three of you, dear," his mother told her. "Trust in God, He is all powerful."

"Come home so we can be with you and help with Lisa," the father-in-law urged.

"No, I will stay here and keep going." But Pattie felt encouraged.

"Remember, mommie," Lisa said, "Daddy said God is there with him. He will come home."

Two weeks before Easter a telegram came saying: "Will arrive at the hospital in Bethesda, on Friday. Hope you can be there."

Pattie felt the sun had never looked brighter, nor the sky bluer, as she and Lisa walked up the steps and in the door of the hospital.

Soon they were in a waiting room and Prince was brought in, in a wheel chair.

"Oh, Prince," was all Pattie could say as she kissed him.

Lisa was a little timid, she had grown a lot in the past year and daddy was still a little bit of a dream to her.

Prince, minus one arm and a leg, with some ugly scars on his face, could only reach out and hold onto one of his loved ones at a time.

"Lisa would you like to ride on my lap?" he asked. Soon she was sitting there with an arm around his neck.

"Pattie, you are as pretty as the day I met you," he told his wife.

92

"Oh, Prince it has been so horrible." She began to cry.

"The worst is over now," he told her. "I will be in and out of hospitals until I get a Government issued leg and arm, but I am going home with you for a few weeks now. I'll go with you and Lisa to Easter services if you will let me."

"Just a day or two and I will get to go for a few days."

As Pattie and Lisa left at the close of visiting hours, they met a pretty young woman going down the steps.

"Is your husband badly hurt?" Pattie asked her.

"Well, he sure doesn't look like the guy I said goodbye to." The girl sounded cross. "I'm going home today and start divorce proceedings."

"Oh, no, that would be so cruel!" Pattie exclaimed.

"Cruel or not, I don't intend to be tied down."

At the hotel Pattie found Prince's parents had just arrived. They were eager to go to the hospital but knew they would have to wait until visiting hours.

"Oh, mom, I'll take care of him, if we can just get him home," Pattie told her mother-in-law.

"We never doubted your love and loyalty for a moment," the mother said. "We are so proud of the brave way you have carried on."

Easter Sunday found Pattie busy dressing her husband. Pinning up the empty sleeve and pants leg, petting him and feeling happy. Lisa in new clothes pranced about, glad to have a male audience.

Then they were in the little church, a small family, grateful to be together again.

The minister walked back to Prince's wheel chair and pushed it to the front.

"This dear man is going to tell us how God saved his life, and allowed him to come home."

In simple sincere words Prince told the audience how he had always, since a young boy, trusted completely in God.

"I felt the presence of the Father on the battle front, and

I prayed for Him to care for my loved ones, for often I felt they were in danger at home."

The minister then preached a sermon on the sufferings of Christ and the victorious coming forth from the grave.

As the people left the church Prince and his family had to wait because of the clumsy chair. The minister came to help get him out.

Suddenly Pattie began to sob. "What is it my dear?" the minister asked.

"I do not know the God Prince talks about. I want to be born again also."

"It is at last the answer to my prayers," Prince said as he wiped away the tears with his one good hand.

"What is wrong with mommie?" Lisa asked.

"She is like the pretty flowers coming up in the yard," Prince told her. "Mommie is finding new life in Christ Jesus."

Pattie knelt by the chair and put her head on Prince's chest. "I always wanted to believe, I just lost sight of the good for awhile."

23

Glad Hearts Look Ahead
(New Year)

"So teach us to number our days, that we may apply our hearts unto wisdom." — Psalm 90:12

Mrs. Tracey sat in front of her class, ten women in their late forties. The lesson was on prayer and she very much wanted each member to grow as a Christian during the year they were about to start.

"We will start with Annie, and I want each of you to tell some way God has answered prayer in your life during the year just past." Mrs. Tracy leaned back to listen.

"Oh, I think I have had such a nice year," Annie said. "I had prayed for my husband to get a job here in town and stop being a traveling man. He is so settled in his new job. Our home is so different and happy."

Virgina was next in line, "My son was in Germany and I was afraid some terrible thing would happen to him." Tears filled her eyes. "I know I prayed more this year than ever before. Now he is on the way home."

Katie, the jolly one, spoke next, "I have asked all of you to pray for my sister because she had such serious illness. She is not well, but thanks to prayer, she is on the road to recovery."

On around the circle they went, some with more to be grateful for than others, until they came to Jaxie.

"Oh, Mrs. Tracey, you know my days are numbered," she looked around the circle at her friends. "How can I say my prayers have been answered when I have to go to the hospital and take those cobalt treatments?"

Mrs. Tracey looked at her pupil. "You do face a problem, but I remember some answered prayers."

The women looked at their teacher. To them it seemed Jaxie was brave just to attend class. She had a malignant tumor. The tumor had been removed but the doctors told her they were sure some malignancy was left in her body. Perhaps six months or a year at most and she would be gone.

"Last year in January we were all praying God would let you live until spring, to see your daughter graduate from school. God granted our prayers." Mrs. Tracey smiled. "Now we are all beginning a new year, our days for this year are numbered. No matter how ill or how strong and well you are, each must face a responsibility for making this the best year of their lives."

"I will probably not be able to attend class too many more times," Jaxie smiled. "Will each of you come and visit me? I will dedicate my last months to praying for you and your problems."

"I will dedicate this year of my life to help Jaxie with her home problems," Annie spoke up.

"There is one thing that bothers me most of all," Jaxie said. "My daughter will have no mother to help her when it comes to the time to get married."

"Some of us may go before you do Jaxie," Mrs. Tracey spoke quietly, "but we pledge here and now to stand by your child when she needs us."

The class closed by holding hands and each saying a prayer of gratitude for the past and asking blessings for the future.

Our days are numbered and yet we enter each New Year

as if we had all the time in the world to accomplish the tasks we have been assigned.

In Job 32:7, we read three words, "Days should speak."

When we stand on the threshold of a New Year we are filled with plans, desires, and hopes for a better time to come. The tramp, tramp, and plod, plod, of the past year is going away into history, now we face a new future.

If we determine to make each day speak, we will be more alert to new opportunities in new directions. If we let each day speak we will begin to question ourselves about how our day speaks. Are we gaining chances to grow, to win others, to be unselfish?

A young man, always impatient and impulsive, gave his parents much cause for concern. In place of having the theory that life is for the glory of God, the young man thought life was for his own gratification.

After one of his impatient outbursts at something being so slow in coming, his father made a suggestion.

"Go on a trip and climb a mountain. Bring me back a rock from the top."

"I will start tomorrow!" the boy exclaimed.

"Well, shouldn't you take time to plan what you will need, bed rolls, food, ropes, picks?" the father asked.

The boy was soon engrossed in planning his trip. A friend decided to go with him. The two boys read everything they could find on mountain climbing. They made a careful list of supplies needed.

The parents taking a vacation camped at the foot of the mountain to wait and watch. The boys thought they could climb to the top in two days.

The mountain was not too high and the climb not too difficult. The father had seen to that. The first night the boys were able to find a nice, wide place to make camp. Being boys and hungry, they ate, and then ate some more. Next morning they had barely enough food left for breakfast. The climb the second day was much harder because they had no food at noon time.

At last, late in the afternoon, they reached the top. There they found their parents had broken camp and driven around and up a road to wait for them.

"Well, what did you learn?" the father asked as they sat around a campfire eating.

"We learned not to eat everything at one meal."

"We learned we had to keep going forward, we couldn't go back."

"We learned we climbed just one step at a time."

"You have accomplished much," the man told the boys, "Life is lived one day at a time. All the good cannot be enjoyed in one day or one year. After a day is passed you cannot go back over it and correct your mistakes."

"And if we just keep climbing, there will be some food at the top." The boys laughed.

A New Start

As the New Year's bells are pealing,
Down into my heart are stealing
Thoughts of joyous hopes and healing
    In a thrilling, fresh, new start.

It's a grand and glorious feeling
In a world so sick and reeling,
When you find your soul down kneeling
    As it seeks a hopeful part.

Then the way ahead's appealing
When you find that God's revealing
His great love and not concealing
    He has granted a new start.
        — J. T. Bolding

24

Thanksgiving Is in the Heart

*"The lines are fallen unto me in pleasant places; yea,
I have a goodly heritage."* — Psalm 16:6

At the beginning of World War II, Tom King was a young
man with a problem. He had a twisted, cripple foot. He was
unfit for military service. He lived on a small farm and his
father thought he was a good farmer.

As Tom watched other boys his age leave and go into the
military service, he wanted to do more for his country than
stay on the farm.

He went to Grand Prairie, Texas, and secured a position
in a plant there. The plant was making needed supplies for
the armed forces.

Tom enjoyed living in such a busy atmosphere. He found
a doctor in nearby Dallas who would operate on his foot and
at least make him walk more normally.

Indeed Tom did feel the lines of life had fallen upon him
in pleasant places when he met and married a nice young
woman.

According to the popular custom of the times, they made
a down payment on a new home and settled down to enjoying the comforts of life.

Life went along and two children came to their home
and they were proud and happy indeed.

Tom and Sue never went to church. After all, he worked all week. On Sunday there were things to fix about the house or garden. Then the children liked to go to the Zoo in Dallas on Sundays, or to a ball game. Church was just not in their program.

Once in awhile someone came by visiting from one of the local churches. They were not intentionally rude to the church visitors, but often they failed even to turn the television set down, in order to carry on a conversation.

"Why do we need the church," Tom would say. "We have our home, our children. I have a job. They just want us to go and give money."

It was nearing Thanksgiving time in 1968, when Tom stopped to pick up his middle of the month check from the paymaster.

He just stuck the envelope in his coat pocket and started home, by way of a popular hangout place for the workers.

Soon after he settled back to enjoy his cold drink, one of the other workers in his department came in.

"Tom, did you get a pink slip?" he asked.

"Why, I never thought of such a thing." Tom reached for his envelope. "Did you get one?"

"Yes, two hundred men were turned off, contracts are running out." The man told him.

Tom hastily opened his pay envelope. Yes, there it was, he would not be needed after the next week.

At home Tom and Sue discussed their plight, payments to meet on almost everything, from washing machine to car. In the years past they had not denied themselves or the children anything.

"Well, I can go over into the city of Dallas and find some work," Tom assured his wife.

Days passed and Tom could find nothing. He had moved to the city from a farm and he was not trained for any type of work, except that which he had learned in the plant.

The day before Thanksgiving, weary and discouraged Tom came home to find Sue crying.

"Don't cry, Sue, I'll find something yet." He did not feel the assurance he tried to show.

"Tomorrow is Thanksgiving and we have nothing to be thankful for," she sobbed.

"Will we have a turkey?" the children asked.

"Not this year," Sue replied.

"I am planning a big surprise, better than a turkey," Tom told them. He sounded more confident than he felt.

Next morning the children were up early. "What is the surprise?" they cried.

"We are going to take a picnic lunch and drive to a place in the country where I lived when I was your age," Tom explained.

"I guess that will show Billy Smith!" said little Tom. "His mother said we couldn't have Thanksgiving. She said only people with churches could be thankful."

Tom felt heavyhearted as they drove along the road, going the hundred miles to his old community. He felt a need for the security he had felt as a boy growing up. The past twenty years he had been too busy to go back very often.

The leaves were red and brown on the trees along the way, the sun was shining as the sun does so often in the East Texas fall time. The day seemed perfect, except Tom had no money, no job, no hopes.

The children were enjoying the new sights and sounds of the rural countryside.

Suddenly they topped a hill and there on the side of the road they saw a white church, it's steeple pointing toward the heavens.

Tom stopped the car. "There, that is my church," he exclaimed. "I went there every Sunday, until I left home to go to work in Dallas."

"Let's get out, we want to see it." The children were out of the car in a flash. They ran to peep in the windows.

Tom walked toward the small cemetery where his parents lay buried for many years.

"We might just as well eat our lunch here," Sue called.

Coming back from the graves of his parents Tom stopped at the church window and began to explain to the children the things they could see.

When Sue called them to come and eat, Tom did not seem to be hungry. In his mind's eye he was remembering one hot August night during a revival many years before. He saw again a small country boy in overalls, walk down to the front of the battered old pulpit and the minister who stood waiting. Tom had been that boy. He had given his heart and life to Christ that night. He remembered the happy tears of his parents and neighbors.

No wonder he had lost his job. No wonder even the next door neighbor said they could have no Thanksgiving. He had forgotten the worthwhile things in life.

Tom got up from the picnic spread on the cloth before him and walked back to the window of the church. Looking in at the same old pulpit he uttered a prayer, "God forgive me for these wasted years. Help me to find a way to support my family and I will see that they have a chance to know you."

As they were cleaning up after the picnic lunch and about to get in the car, an elderly man driving a very old and wheezy pickup stopped.

"Howdy, folks," he spoke in the accustomed greeting of the community.

"Hello —" Tom automatically said. "Why if it isn't Lem Taylor! How are you, I'm Tom King."

"Well, Tom, it's been a spell since we have seen you around these parts."

The two men chatted for a few moments, the children crowding close to examine the old old car.

As the old man started up his motor he said: "Tom, you'd best go see your Uncle Ned, he is sick."

"Yes, we will go there next."

So they drove to a prosperous looking farm not too many miles from the church.

Tom's uncle and aunt were so glad to see him and meet his family.

Noticing out of the window how the children were going about looking at everything, the old man looked at Tom and said, "Tom, why don't you come back home and work my farm next year? Those children don't need to grow up in the city, a plain unhealthy place. You and your wife both look peaked."

"Do you mean that Uncle Ned?" Tom's heart gave a sudden pound inside his chest.

"Sure do mean it. You know my boys all own bigger farms over in the next county. I want to retire." The old man sighed, "I'm just plain worn out and your aunt wants to live in the village."

"I would need to go home and sell my house," Tom told him, "but we could be moved here by Christmas."

"Now, Tom, you always were a good boy. I knew when you drove up God had sent me some help."

Then as the old often do, the man and woman started talking to each other about where they would live in the village.

Late that afternoon a tired little family drove into their driveway at Grand Prairie.

Little Tom and his sister almost ran over each other as they started running towards the neighbor's house.

"Billy, Billy," they called, "We found us a church and we are going to move. It will be our church."

Sue looked at Tom. "We had a nice Thanksgiving after all."

"Yes, Sue, God is so good and I have been so ungrateful." Tom picked up the picnic basket. "I'll try to make it up to the children for my neglect. They shall have a church."

"Tom, I never had a church either," Sue walked with her arm around her husband's waist.

"Food and clothing can't take the place of God and a Thanksgiving in the heart."

Gratitude

True gratitude is born in those
    Who take the time to count
Their blessings rather than their woes,
    Rejoicing as they mount.

God's mercies are so very great:
    Abundant is his care;
On him we never have to wait
    For he is always there.

True joy becomes a way of life
    For those whose eyes will see
God's providence 'mid toil and strife
    Bestowed on us for free.
            — J. T. Bolding